Between Day and Night

BETWEEN DAY AND NIGHT

New and Selected Poems 1946-2010

Miguel González-Gerth

Edited by David A. Colón

Library of Congress Cataloging-in-Publication Data

Gonzalez-Gerth, Miguel.
Between day and night : new and selected poems, 1946-2010 / Miguel González-Gerth ; edited by David A. Colón.
p. cm.
Poems in both English and Spanish.
1. Gonzalez-Gerth, Miguel--Interviews. 2. Poets, American--20th century--Interviews. 3. Poets, American--21st century--Interviews. 4. Bilingual authors--Texas--Interviews. I. Colón, David A. II. Title.
PQ7298.17.O459B48 2013
811'.54--dc23
2012039697

TCU Press
P.O. Box 298300
Fort Worth, Texas 76129
817.257.7822
www.prs.tcu.edu

To order books: 1.800.826.8911

Designed by fusion29.com

Contents

Foreword

Artists who dare to create anew take risks. Some choose to do so paradoxically—within recognizable constraints. Those who do so within the formal constraints of poetry seem to risk it all. Already working within an aesthetic form with fewer and fewer readers, those who reinvent within tradition experience a certain cold shoulder from those among the so-called avant-garde who throw form to the wind.

With the publication of *Between the Day and Night: New and Selected Poems 1946-2010*, David A. Colón brings to the English-reading world one of the twentieth century's greatest unsung formalist innovators, Miguel González-Gerth. In the "Author's Note" to *Looking for the Horse Latitudes* (2007), González-Gerth remarks that his lifetime of dedication to the writing of poetry "in all ways imaginable" . . . "allows me to think and feel and say whatever flows through my brain and the rest of my nervous system" (iv). He is a self-identified "ambilingual" poet, comfortable creating in Spanish and English, who builds scaffolding of the recognizable (sonnet or pantoum, for instance) absorbed into the new (X, Y, Z) to create new wondrous edifices. He is an artist who recreates from paradox—the new within the old—proving that there are no limits to formalist poetry well done. But writing formalist poetry, as he remarks, cost him "the attention of many a publisher" (iv). His poetry insists on our considering poetry not as shaped by repetition, meter, rhyme, line-cut alone, nor theme, but rather as an organic system of interrelated subsystems. Time and time again, with González-Gerth's poems we find a particular aesthetic pleasure in the way his sculpting corresponds aesthetically to the content; we feel good soaking up the form together with its contents.

When Miguel González-Gerth creates, he adds something new to the world. Of course, his poems refer both to the lofty and the banal (from philosophical meditation to anything under the sun), but always in ways that reorient our vision, thought, and feeling about the subject. In the final quatrain of his four stanza rhymed poem "Art of Poetry," his poet-speaker remarks: "Poetry, I now think, must be reality's chagrin, / An impunctilious trespass as original as sin. / Poetic art is soft as silk and cutting as a knife / And every poem a tender blow against the chains of life" (*The Musicians and Other Poems,* 27). González-Gerth's point of departure and arrival is: the *poem as a poem*. Moreover, his poetry refers to life just as it trespasses, then transcends its territory as something new in the world. This something new that he creates asks that we as readers of and listeners to his poetry experience all variety of new sensations, thoughts, and feelings as they relate to the graspably concrete or the fleetingly fluid.

Recently I spent time with a coterie of a newer generation of formalist poets of Latino ethnic descent. While there was a surge of poets in the 1980s who chose to use the constraints of formal metrical verse technique and rhyme in their poetry, with few exceptions most were non-Latino. Why, I wondered? This was the time of the so-called "poetry wars" when the use of formal technique was considered retrograde—even ideologically conservative. Yet, Dana Gioia and other champions of what was called the New Formalism fought back with pen as sword, reminding the world that form in and of itself was not "intrinsically good or bad" (*Can Poetry Matter?,* 30).

Recall that Latino poetry during this period was still heavy under the influence of the post-civil rights Brown Power movement. This was a poetry of resistance—and written mostly in free verse; written deliberately free of structure as such to purportedly throw off any Western-identified mind-forged shackles. (For more on this epoch, see Juan Bruce-Novoa's *Chicano Poetry: A Response to Chaos,* Marta E. Sánchez's *Contemporary Chicana Poetry*, and Rafael Pérez-Torres's *Movements in Chicano Poetry*.) For Latino poets, this was a salient moment. I focused my efforts on poets such as Rafael Campo, C. Dale Young, Rhina Espaillat, and Julia Alvarez, who simply chose formal convention and not ideological prescription.

I chose to spend my time with them as I would a series of skilled carpenters—to see how tools could be used to fashion all sorts of three, four, five legged tables. Just as a carpenter of furniture makes tables, a poet, as Borges would say, *makes poems*. Just as the carpenter needs tools—and needs to know how to use them—to transform (cut, shave, notch, glue, screw) her raw materials into something stable that we might use to write or eat at, so too does the poet need tools to transform his or her raw material (the infinite facets of reality) into something we might read or hear with an aesthetic delight. She is a maker of an artifact built with tools that are appropriate for the trade and that enable the realization of something with a specific purpose in the world: a spatially designed, purposefully segmented visual/aural artifact that steers the imagination, emotion, thought, and perception into new territories. González-Gerth is another such carpenter. Like those I have spent hours with of late, he too takes an idea or image, works it over in the mind, then skillfully uses different tools to make it physically present in the form of poetry. Indeed, as Colón shows us clearly herein, González-Gerth has been publishing lasting poetry since just after World War II. That is, he's been in the game long before Campo, Young, Espaillat, and Alvarez. Or should we say, rather, that he's been composing, in Colón's words, "not so much in the borderland but on the frontiers of the borderland, and—in equal quantities—in the extremes of Spanish and English and the distinct literary traditions of Anglo-America and Latin America." Retrospectively and with Colón's guidance, we should consider González-Gerth from here on out as one of the forefathers of a Latino *ambilingual* poetic tradition visible at the edges of our cultural borderlands. We should consider him part of a Latino poetic tradition whereby the deliberate synergistic interplay of form and content aim carefully to trigger new sensations, thoughts, and feelings in the listeners and readers.

And, just as we might (and do) judge the carpenter's table as well done or not, so too do we judge the poet as competent or not. Indeed, we read line by line but we absorb as a whole. When this is done well, as with González-Gerth's work herein, we smile with our ears and cheer with our eyes. When not done well, and the poem can be quite fragile here, losing its balance with the wrong choice of rhyme, line, or word, it can be heard as a screech to our mind's ear. As David Colón so beautifully illustrates by taking the poet and his poetry seriously, we return again and again, do we not, to those that create a sense of *awe* in their unity of parts that make a whole like those poems of Miguel González-Gerth.

Frederick Luis Aldama
Arts & Humanities Distinguished Professor of English
The Ohio State University

Books Cited

Aldama, Frederick Luis. *Formal Matters in Contemporary Latino Poetry*. New York: Palgrave, 2013.

González-Gerth, Miguel. *Looking for the Horse Latitudes*. Austin: Host Publications, 2007.

—. *The Musicians and Other Poems*. Austin: University of Texas, 2001.

Gioia, Dana. *Can Poetry Matter?: Essays on Poetry and American Culture*. Saint Paul: Graywolf Press, 1992.

Bruce-Novoa, Juan. *Chicano Poetry: A Response to Chaos*. Austin: University of Texas Press, 1982.

Sánchez, Marta E. *Contemporary Chicana Poetry*. Berkeley: University of California Press, 1986.

Pérez-Torres, Rafael. *Movements in Chicano Poetry: Against Myths, Against Margins*. Cambridge: Cambridge University Press, 1995.

Acknowledgments

The editor wishes to thank Alex Lemon, Francisco Aragón, Dan Williams, David Vanderwerken, Theresa Gaul, and Daniel Juan Gil for advice and feedback on this project throughout its various stages of development. He also wishes to thank Tita Valencia for providing valuable contributions as amanuensis. Funding for the research on this project was provided by a Research and Creative Activities Fund (RCAF) grant from Texas Christian University. The editor offers his sincerest thanks to RCAF Committee Chair Peter Worthing, Dean of AddRan College of Liberal Arts Andrew Schoolmaster, and Associate Provost/Dean of University Programs Bonnie Melhart.

The editor also wishes to acknowledge the following journals and magazines for having previously published certain poems contained in these pages: the *Dirty Goat*, the *Lawrentian*, the *New York Times Book Review*, *Nimrod*, and *Poetry at the University of Texas*.

Introduction

Eight months after his historic flight from New York to Paris, Charles Lindbergh landed his one-man plane at Balbuena Field in Mexico City on the afternoon of December 14, 1927. The Lone Eagle had departed from the US capital the prior day intent on performing a goodwill mission of diplomacy. Tens of thousands of enthusiastic onlookers greeted the American hero, as did numerous distinguished statesmen, including Ambassador Dwight Whitney Morrow, President Plutarco Elías Calles, and General Miguel González Cadena, head of Mexico's department of aviation. The reception was propitious, for Lindbergh's stay in Mexico was spectacular. He toured the region as a celebrity. He was awarded the key to Mexico City by its mayor. He even began a relationship with Morrow's daughter Anne that would eventually lead to marriage. The spirit of goodwill expanded through reciprocity, and on the second day of his visit, Lindbergh granted an extraordinary invitation to General González Cadena: the aviator offered his plane for a flight around the city. The General accepted, but responded with an equally curious request: that his baby son come, too. So goes this family fable—that Miguel González-Gerth, barely old enough to walk, took to the sky in the world's most famous airplane, soaring above the site of Tenochtitlan in *The Spirit of St. Louis*.

A well-earned, august tale. And as it pertains to subsequent events in the life of González-Gerth—who has lived in Mexico, Spain, and the United States and has produced a diverse oeuvre of poetry in English and in Spanish that spans eight decades—its premise is fittingly symbolic. González-Gerth himself suggests as much, in his poem "Lindbergh":

Not Trismegistus but the god
You now resemble in my mind,
So unhermetic yet so odd:
A scene left fifty years behind.

An ocean, now compressed in time

And space where orbiting machines
Turn the ridiculous sublime,
Painted your portrait in blue-greens.

The great flight overcame balloons.
A journey south good will enhanced.
Blind to Icarian afternoons
I was uniquely circumstanced:

Your Spirit bade me share its deeds,
Aloft the wind charged every bend.
Now it's false memory that leads
Me, like winged Hermes, to my end.

The poem elevates the legend of flying aboard *The Spirit of St. Louis* with religious undertones, yet seems aware of the story's unlikelihood by admitting "false memory." The allusion to classical mythology as well as the formalist prosody—iambs, tetrameter, rhyme—are fairly common in González-Gerth's poetry, as is the manner in which they are employed. "Lindbergh" belongs to that body of González-Gerth's poetry written in his acquired language and exhibits how he, whether or not memory is the point of departure, approaches composing English poems far more as a process of construction than as a means to expression. The meticulous, formal, Romantic language and tone might seem appropriate for homage to Lindbergh the great historical figure, but the root of the poem is a childhood experience. For González-Gerth, since English is not his native language, the sense of formality when composing in English is always there to some extent, even in confessional mode. Branching out from this foundation, González-Gerth consistently produces poems that combine extremes: distance and proximity, nature and abstraction, discipline and abandon. In the case of "Lindbergh," history is crossed with anecdote, mythology with experience. Lindbergh is likened to Hermes and thus deified, and yet the address of the "I" to a "you" is very personal. It suggests a kinship between Lindbergh and the speaker, bringing the two subjects down to earth, so to speak, in the way the poem hints that they may share more.

Like Lindbergh, González-Gerth was the son of a prominent leader. Miguel González Cadena joined the Mexican Revolution in 1913 at the age of twenty-two and climbed Mexico's military ranks swiftly, in part because of his success in commanding troops in battle, to retire as a major general who had served on important international commissions. Like Lindbergh, González-Gerth began his college career intent on studying engineering, loyally following his father's path. Like Lindbergh, González-Gerth dedicated himself to the cause of improving Anglo-Hispanic relations—Lindbergh in the arena of politics, González-Gerth in the humanities, through his fifty-year career in the United States as professor, translator, critic, and poet.

And like Lindbergh, González-Gerth has always been an individualist. The metaphor of a one-man mission is apt for considering González-Gerth the poet. His aesthetic and tone, born from his taste for British Romantics and the Spanish Generation of '27, mark much of his poetry as formalist. Standing against the current of emergent modernisms and aesthetic movements that required a wholesale commitment to either an ideology or a scene, González-Gerth has never been a social poet. Perhaps it was for his style, a unique blend of Romantic, confessional, and *modernista*; perhaps for his modesty, as he has published mostly in Texas and Mexico; or perhaps it has been because of his cultural identity, for he writes in both Spanish and English and is a Mexican citizen living in Texas but has allied himself with neither Chicano literary currents nor trends in contemporary Mexican poetry. As González-Gerth himself has said, "I'm only on the edge of tradition. . . . I don't really have a tradition that is fixed and recognizable." Like Lindbergh, González-Gerth the poet has, more often than not, flown solo.

Miguel González-Gerth was born in Mexico City on August 15, 1926. His mother, Claire Esther Gerth, was one of eight children born to a Mexican mother and a German father, an immigrant from a town near Dresden who first moved to the United States to work for the American Smelting and Refining Company but later settled in central Mexico. Gerth studied at the National Conservatory of Music in Mexico and was a talented pianist, though she would forego a career in music to marry and to raise her three children. Nevertheless, she maintained for her children a learning environment steeped in the arts—she often played piano at home, pursued an amateur interest in ballet, and encouraged her eldest son Miguel to read literature, especially Latin American and Mexican poets.

One such poet was a member of the family. González-Gerth's uncle, Ricardo López Méndez, was the director of the Public Library in Yucatán and a radio pioneer who penned many famous lyrics, including "*Amor, Amor, Amor*," a song translated into English and recorded by Bing Crosby. López Méndez made a more lasting literary impression with "Credo" (1941), a deeply patriotic twelve-stanza lyric poem González-Gerth calls "an invocation of Mexico itself." "Credo" was meant to galvanize intellectual support for President Lázaro Cárdenas in his effort to expropriate oil from British, US, and Dutch companies operating in Mexico. The anaphoristic poem deftly works arresting imagery into propaganda, as, for example, in the tenth stanza:

México, creo en ti,
como creo en los clavos que te sangran,
en las espinas que hay en tu corona,
y en el mar que te aprieta la cintura
para que tomes en la forma humana
hechura de sirena en las espumas.

(Mexico, I believe in you,
as I believe in the nails that make you bleed,
in the thorns that are in your crown,
and in the sea that tightens around your waist
squeezing you into the human form
of a siren in sea foam.) [Ed.]

While the political purpose and overt Christian allegory of this poem are features rarely seen in González-Gerth's oeuvre, classical metonymy and the evocation of nature as sentient are ideas that have served his palette throughout the years. González-Gerth cites López Méndez as an early influence, especially for his poetry's lyricism and "epic tonality." In fact, when asked about his literary influences, González-Gerth speaks of his family before listing his favorite poets. His mother, a Presbyterian, was a creative force of style and grace; his father, the engineer, career military man, and agnostic, preferred the discipline of history.

González-Gerth's childhood was privileged, and he traveled extensively. When he was five, his family moved to El Paso, Texas and lived comfortably there for some time before moving back over the border when his father was assigned to command the garrison in Juárez. A year later the family returned to Mexico City, and González-Gerth enrolled in a British school where he was first exposed to English language, literature, and history. In 1934, the family moved again, this time to Spain, where his father was to negotiate the procurement of vessels for the Mexican coast guard. The family spent several days in New York City before sailing to Southampton on their way to Madrid. González-Gerth recalls his year in Europe as a "process of discovery," taking in "Big Ben and Trafalgar Square, Napoleon's tomb at Les Invalides, Versailles and the Louvre, the Prado and the Escorial, and the Chancellery on Wilhelmstrasse" when just nine years old. Before the Spanish Civil War began in 1936, the family went back to Mexico, and González-Gerth returned to his British school with a newfound appreciation for English literature ignited by the firsthand experiences of his travels.

However, "the definitive border crossing, both geographical and cultural," for González-Gerth came in 1940, when he was sent to attend the Texas Military Institute (TMI) in San Antonio. At this time his father established a cattle ranch in northern Mexico, with a view of Big Bend National Park across the river, and traveling back and forth between Mexico and the United States thereafter became routine. At TMI, he began composing stories and poems in English, imitating Edgar Allan Poe and Robert Louis Stevenson, trying his hand at rondeaux and rondels. In his four years at TMI, González-Gerth's literary aspirations took hold, and the chances of him following in his father's footsteps as an engineer began to dwindle.

After two years working in Mexico for his uncle, González-Gerth crossed the border again and enrolled, in 1947, at the University of Texas at Austin—a year after he published his first monograph of poetry, a modest chapbook containing a single poem called *Aquarelle: The Calendar in Verse*, with Editorial Clásica in Mexico City. In spite of this work, González-Gerth spent the next two years pursuing a degree in engineering before he switched, with permission from his parents, to modern languages. Among many teachers at the University of Texas who greatly impressed him, three had the most lasting influence on his tastes and perspective as a poet: Robert Clarence Stephenson, Willis Pratt, and Ramón Martínez-López. Stephenson, an English professor, exposed González-Gerth to the possibilities of comparative literature before it was recognized as an academic field, putting French, Russian, Spanish, and English literatures into conversation—González-Gerth recalls Stephenson's course in Proust as a particular favorite. Another favorite was Pratt's course in Romantic poetry. It was in this setting that González-Gerth devoted himself to reading Byron, Shelley, Keats, Hunt, Wordsworth, and Coleridge, the pillars of Romanticism whom he would honor with the sincerest form of flattery. In 1950, González-Gerth won the Creative Writing Prize at the University of Texas, and his portfolio's capstone poem, "To Spring: An Ode," which he wrote when he was nineteen, is Romantic through and through:

Season of light and soft green renascence,
Child of Diana and Vertumnus born;
Life's day-star that eternally presents
Its youthful spirit to an old world, worn
To near-decay by time, death, hate and war;
Timeless avenger of a timeless grace
Which men ignore who would price all life low;
I challenge them to shatter or debase
The beautiful illusion of your star
Forever brilliant, Spring, oh avatar
Of love, of spirit of youth, eternal glow.

But where is to be found your chrysalis,
Oh Spring? Where blooms the magic of your wings?
You surge forth from the sky, soft as the kiss
Of light, to fall upon and bless all things.
You slowly rise from out the earth and sea,
And cover mountain summits and sea foam
With sleep in wakefulness, the green of hope:
And like the wave returning to its home,
After its journey through the boundless sky,

You are a wave and sleep and cloud, all high
Beyond the feeble grasp of human scope.

Where is the mellow fruit of Autumn's day?
Where, if not nurtured in your warmth of song?
For you bring back to life the breath and clay
That, past oblivion, doubt and death, have long
Inhabited this earth, as if they seek
To render homage for a glad surprise.
You are the spark to which our spirit clings,
The smile we lift to heaven, proud or meek,
The promise that we know will crystallize,
Though you may come and go, and in our eyes,
Leave no more than, in air, leave pilgrim wings.

The tone, form, and control of the poem are unmistakably Romantic—the rhetorical interrogatives, the apostrophe, the meter and rhyme—and yet novel turns of phrase (e.g. "Its youthful spirit to an old world, worn" and "After its journey through the boundless sky, / You are a wave and sleep and cloud") seem to make it new. Composed months after the end of the Second World War, the poem contains a youthful feeling of protest ("I challenge them to shatter or debase / The beautiful illusion of your star") that finishes with a surprisingly mature line: "Leave no more than, in air, leave pilgrim wings."

Although one of González-Gerth's earliest poems, "To Spring: An Ode" embodies many of the predominant themes of his work. The personification of nature and the treatment of cycles of time as characters in an ongoing existentialist drama are fixtures of his poetry. His nature poems tend to cast features of landscape as players in a dialectic, addressing questions of emotion, hope, or responsibility. This projection, an act of giving voice to the inanimate or inarticulate, displays traces of Romantic influence but also has roots in González-Gerth's personal experience. As a poet who inhabits two languages and thus is faced with an amplified freedom of verbal expression, he is accustomed to thinking across linguistic divides in pursuit of elusive reconciliations. His verse depictions of the inner struggle of these distinct cultural voices are both aesthetic choices and reflections of character.

The Janus-like quality of his literary sensibility, as a Modernist-era poet looking back to inherited forms to compose new verse, is doubled by his cultural position, facing at once both sides of a border between two countries and two languages. Like Stephenson, Martínez-López steered González-Gerth to studies in comparative literature, advising his master's thesis on "Spanish Themes in American Romantic Literature." As an undergraduate, González-Gerth developed his parallel interests in Spanish and English poetry, allowing both fields to inform each other not only in his academic pursuits but also in his writing. The Mexican poet Ramón López Velarde (1888-1921) had an aesthetic influence on González-Gerth, who shares his tendency in free verse toward spanning many lines of varying lengths with a single, twirling, demanding sentence. Flecks of the Spanish poet Luis Cernuda (1902-1963) show up in González-Gerth's philosophical, declarative statements, especially when infinitives are expressed as universals and ruminations are sustained on emotional themes. Pablo Neruda, too, had his effect on González-Gerth's poetry, expressed most notably through erotic themes and the symbols of night. In his "Love Poem," González-Gerth expands a phrase from Neruda's "*Me gustas cuando callas*" ("I Like You When You're Quiet"), beginning the poem with the line, "I like you when you're speaking" and ending it with, "But I also like you when you're quiet." Such influences distill in González-Gerth's aesthetic, especially in his longer poems composed in free verse. Consider these lines from "The Space of Night," a poem that, in the way it balances narrative impulse with poetic artifice, invokes a style that Alejo Carpentier famously described as "baroque":

Soft chirps revive the sensibility
Of mold, the prototype of crows
That mark the route of migratory flights
Left tattersall on some forsaken map,
Flights much too high for restful sleep
And much too low to manage dreams
Which no one dared to visualize
A million years ago.

The cadence of López Velarde, the darkness of Cernuda, the surrealism of Neruda: González-Gerth has many voices, filtered by a thought process that loops through Spanish and English, allowing for readings that are multiplicitous and intertextual—as well as for a method of composition in which translation is often key. In the above lines, González-Gerth manifests in English aesthetic qualities native to Spanish verse, especially in effecting surprise through the unit of the sentence, not the phrase. But the suggestion of travel and wanderlust in the images of "migratory flights" and "some forsaken map" unites the aesthetic with the narrative. The theme reaches both to language and to experience; the idea of migratory flights, "much too high" yet "much too low," coupled with the enigmatic phrases that begin and end the sentence, raise a sense of indeterminism proportionate both to verbal play and to cultural alienation. In fact, "The Space of Night" was first composed in English, but González-Gerth himself translated the poem into Spanish. The Spanish version is very different from the English, rendered through an approximate, impressionistic process of near-translation, and these quoted lines have no corresponding Spanish equivalent. He claims of the English original, "[c]ertain phrases simply cannot find suitable equivalents" in Spanish. Nevertheless, "The Space of Night" feels like a poem written in English but thought out of Spanish, demonstrating the complexities of González-Gerth's poetry and the emergent possibilities of internalizing cohabitating languages.

As a student at the University of Texas, González-Gerth explored simultaneously the poetic possibilities of both Spanish and English, and in time he would grow his perspective on the relationship between the languages into a theory of translation. While González-Gerth is adamant about not code-switching in his poetry (he calls the practice "schizolingua"), he has self-translated much of his oeuvre in both directions. Many of his poems have experienced a revolving-door migration, passing through phases of development involving interlingual rearticulations. However, González-Gerth preserves the integrity of each language, never venturing into hybrid terrain, and for this he considers himself not a bilingual poet but an "ambilingual" one. This aspect is crucial to his body of work. For González-Gerth, the border in the figurative sense (between English and Spanish), as well as in the literal sense (between Mexico and the United States), has a sovereign identity. It is a definitive circumstance, a factor that extends with equal reach into his poetry and his life.

Oftentimes when reading poets, seeking biography in the poetry can be a fallacy, but regarding González-Gerth, to do so runs less risk of falling into a critical trap. In 1956, González-Gerth published his first collection and married his first wife. It was entitled, *Desert Sequence and Other Poems*; her name was Betty Brumbalow. Betty was Miguel's wife for twenty-six years and would inspire many poems, but *Desert Sequence* contains poems within which earlier memories are transposed. (The chapbook was published by Nonpareil Press in Perth, Western Australia after González-Gerth responded to an advertisement in a literary magazine.) The subtitle of the initial poem is "Summer in the Big Bend National Park," and in three parts the poem conjures images recalled from the poet's experience of the South Texas landscape from the time when his father established his cattle operation on the Rio Grande. The following lines from the first and last stanzas evoke a serene mood as the gaze shifts from west to east, twilight to sunrise, all the while regarding the southern border:

        The sun descends
in layers of luminous air.
Through the Great Window of Chisos,
flanked by austere profiles,
the distance is resonant and misty.
On the other side of the river,
rises a northwest of sierra:
undulant mountains floating nightward
with the incipient dark of evening.
[...]

        Daybreak...!
Dawn winks behind the Rock of Casa Grande;
nebulous firelight glitters
along the burnished contours.
The sun blooms amid the clouds
and kindles distances to iridescence.

The pitch of the poem is attuned to the awesome landscape. And the poem casts vision over "distances" twice in these lines, which can be read two opposite ways: one accounting for the poet's life, the other not. Starting with the latter, the perceptions of distance shrink the self (humanity) within the vastness of nature, effecting humility. In the former, concerns of the living poet come through, as he stands in Big Bend and stares at El Rio, facing his ancestral home on the horizon, inspired and confident. The dusk-to-dawn cycle of the poem is a metonym for a lifetime, but the sense of awe and epiphany doesn't waver, which invokes a Keatsian negative capability: to stand at the portal between two cultures and feel content.

The year *Desert Sequence* was published, González-Gerth took a job to teach at the Lawrenceville School in New Jersey. He moved with Betty and lived in the Northeast for nine years, the first two spent teaching prep school before he began graduate work at Princeton, where he studied under Edmund L. King, Vicente Lloréns, Raymond Willis, R. P. Blackmur, and Don Francisco Ayala. González-Gerth received an MA in 1960 and, while writing his dissertation on the Spanish author Ramón Gómez de la Serna, began teaching at Bryn Mawr, moving on to Haverford and Swarthmore in subsequent years. All the while he continued to write and occasionally published some poems. In December of 1961 and January of 1962, he published three poems from *Desert Sequence* in the *New York Times Book Review*. He composed a twenty-poem sequence, "Essay on Waiting," and published one poem from it in 1964 in the literary quarterly *Approach*. Also in 1964, he privately published an early version of his collection *The Infinite Absence*, with a brief preface by the lauded classicist Richmond Lattimore, a Bryn Mawr colleague, and woodcuts by John Roy. Its brilliant packaging notwithstanding, *The Infinite Absence* enjoyed no critical reception and was out of print in a short time. But it would be revised decades later and republished by the University of Texas to honor the loss of someone González-Gerth cherished.

His years in the Northeast were productive, and the Ivy League proved hospitable. On one occasion he met Harry Levin, the Irving Babbitt Professor of Comparative Literature at Harvard, and the two discussed the option of pursuing a second doctorate under Levin's supervision. But in 1963 González-Gerth's father died, setting in motion a chain of events that would return him to Texas. His widowed mother wanted to settle in Austin, and Betty was responsible for a farm she had inherited in Central Texas. In part for these reasons, González-Gerth accepted an offer from the University of Texas to join the Department of Romance Languages as an Assistant Professor in the fall of 1965.

The two decades following this appointment were a period of professional development for González-Gerth in which he was less productive as a poet than he would be in later years. In 1967 he published a collection of poems in Spanish entitled *En vísperas de olvido* (*On the Eve of Oblivion*), which includes some translations of poems from *Desert Sequence* and which states in its dedication that the poems had been written between 1948 and 1958. In 1969 he joined the staff of the *Texas Quarterly*, ultimately becoming its editor. It was through his work for the *Texas Quarterly* that he would become close friends with Harry Huntt Ransom, Chancellor of the University of Texas and founder of the Humanities Research Center named after him. González-Gerth took a course on Robert Browning with Ransom in the 1950s, and in the summer of 1960 he helped Ransom edit an issue of the *Texas Quarterly* on Spanish history and culture. The relationship grew into a close friendship once González-Gerth had joined the professoriate.

Other important relationships blossomed after González-Gerth had returned to Texas. In 1971, he met Jorge Luis Borges when Borges visited Austin, and after several more visits to Texas over the years by the Argentine master, González-Gerth had become a close enough acquaintance to persuade Borges to sign a letter of bequest promising a collection of handwritten manuscripts as a gift to the Ransom Center. Hazel Ransom has written that the papers were never received "due to incompetence in administrative and legal pursuit or the skillful dissembling by those in possession or both," but the truth remains that Borges and González-Gerth enjoyed a mutually respectful friendship and shared, among other things, a robust appreciation for English poetry.

González-Gerth's most prolific period as a poet came well after he turned fifty and largely because his impulse as a poet is to respond to love and tragedy. In the summer of 1976, González-Gerth traveled to Spain to conduct research, and when he returned he learned his friend Harry

Ransom had died quite unexpectedly. Ransom's widow, Hazel, asked her longtime friend to help her prepare and edit Ransom's uncollected writings, and in the years that followed, she and González-Gerth worked closely to publish several posthumous volumes: *The Conscience of the University and Other Essays* (1982); *The Other Texas Frontier* (1984); *Snow in Austin: A Collection of Photographs from 1895 to 1985* (1986); *The Song of Things Begun* (1988), a collection of verse; and *Chronicles of Opinion on Higher Education, 1955-1975* (1990).

Before any of these books appeared in print, Betty fell gravely ill. She was diagnosed with a brain tumor, and died of the cancer in 1982. At a time when his daily work was a constant reminder of the loss of his close friend Harry, González-Gerth was toppled by grief over the death of his wife. In response, he revived the manuscript *The Infinite Absence*, originally composed some thirty years earlier, and published the revised version, dedicated to Betty's memory, in an ambilingual format through the University of Texas in 1984. The collection presents Spanish and English versions of each poem *en face*, his first ambilingual collection, effecting what he suggests might be considered "a confluence of poetic expression, a bilingual idiom." But perhaps what is more remarkable about the volume is how prescient it was when first written and published decades earlier. Stylistically, the poems in *La ausencia infinita / The Infinite Absence* diverge from González-Gerth's neo-Romantic mode, taking form in short snippets (at times reminiscent of William Carlos Williams's early poems and the variable foot), while expressing a solemn despair so befitting the emotions he would feel from his wife's death it's almost uncanny:

CEGUEDAD

Mis pupilas han volado hacia el vacío
Y han desgranado sus últimas miradas
Sobre las íntimas moradas
De mis sueños

Ciego, ¿qué habré de sentir
Ahora que los huecos de la noche
Se han llenado

De indescriptibles cosas?
Las ascuas nocturnas ya no irán
Por las sendas de mi ensueño
Y apenas mi corazón contemplará
El arco iris de mis lágrimas

BLINDNESS

My eyes have flown toward the void
And have shed their final gaze
Over the intimate dwellings
Of my dreams

Blind, what will I feel
Now that the crevasses of the night
Have become filled
With indescribable things?

Nocturnal embers will no longer
Follow the path of my fancy
And my heart will behold only
The rainbow of my weeping

Typical of all the poems in *La ausencia infinita/The Infinite Absence*, the translation is direct and literal. Only the first two lines of the final stanza pose any challenge to preserving the lineation of syntax—the rest of the translation is as unsurprising as the poem itself is metaphorical. *The Infinite Absence* certainly stands apart from the rest of González-Gerth's oeuvre, mainly for its looseness of form and slightly less for its somber tenor. Besides republishing *The Infinite Absence*, González-Gerth composed a new series of daily poems in response to Betty's death entitled *Palabras inútiles* (*Useless Words*), published in Madrid in 1988. Unlike *The Infinite Absence*, *Palabras inútiles* is composed entirely in Spanish, with no parallel English versions of the poems. González-Gerth has explained that this happened, in a manner of speaking, out of his control. He has stated that English, as a language he acquired after being brought up in Spanish, is "less natural" for him—in his own words, he admits that in English, "I tend to be more careful . . . and because of that, I tend to be more inventive," whereas in Spanish, "I let language lead me." The death of Betty was a loss so emotionally profound that the right words came to him only in Spanish, and they are indeed challenging to render suitably into English. *Palabras inútiles* nevertheless shares much with *The Infinite Absence* vis-à-vis darkness, lament, and solitude, as can be seen in these lines from "*5 de marzo*":

> *Vivir es difícil cuando no se tiene un norte,*
> *cuando se ha perdido el alma,*
> *cuando no se encuentra el nido.*
> *Mi nido está vacío,*
> *mi alma está perdida,*
> *y en vez de norte tengo*
> *el fragor de los días.*
>
> (Living is hard when there's no point,
> once the soul has disappeared,
> when home is gone.
> My nest is empty,
> my soul is lost,
> and instead of purpose I have
> the din of days.) [Ed.]

The weight of solemnity in these poems is achieved by layers of images reflecting the evanescence endemic to nature: movement, cycles, death and waiting. The tribute to Betty looms on every page. But in the years between the book's composition in 1982-1983 and its publication in 1988, the collection took on added meaning. González-Gerth's mother, Claire Esther Gerth, died in 1985. In retrospect, it seems that *Palabras inútiles*, not unlike *The Infinite Absence*, is a book González-Gerth wrote once but felt twice.

William Carlos Williams once remarked, "Determined women have governed my fate." While to say the same of González-Gerth might not be perfectly true, he did have a number of relationships with ambitious, talented, and sophisticated women who served him as muses to some degree or another. His 1991 collection, *The Musicians and Other Poems*, is full of poems dedicated to or inspired by many real women, and even some imagined. One imagined woman is "The Country Nurse":

Barbed wire fences round the haybarn lots
Retained the semblance of the former toil
Leading toward the farm house, a human foil
At twilight. A window showed disheveled cots,
Prolific as black soil showered in spring,
Where unemployment in late awakening
Compromised industry. And everywhere
The space was dead, dismal the air.
The feeling there was one of hopelessness.
She left the doorway framed in grief.
She smiled and waved, felt like a thief,
Instead of one who has made sorrow less.

The real women include, among others, Katherine Wheatley, one of González-Gerth's early college teachers; an anonymous "Pregnant Girl With Dogs"; his mother; his college sweetheart, Clara; and Hazel Ransom. After Betty died in 1982 and González-Gerth had begun to work with Hazel to edit her late husband's unpublished works, the friendship between González-Gerth and Hazel grew into romance, and the two enjoyed a decade of fruitful companionship. The couple succeeded in augmenting Harry Ransom's authorial legacy, and González-Gerth himself continued to enjoy professional success at the University of Texas, being promoted to Professor in 1987.

When Hazel died of breast cancer in 1993, González-Gerth served as her executor, overseeing her generous donation to the Harry Ransom Humanities Research Center as well as the publication of her collection of fiction, *A Vacation in the Sun and Other Stories* (1996), and her master's thesis, *Elizabeth Barrett Browning: Poet-Reformer* (1997). Both of these volumes were published by the University of Texas, as was González-Gerth's tribute to Hazel, a chapbook entitled *Poems to Hazel* (1994). Of the four poems in this monograph, the poem "Sic Transit" is most compassionate. It suggests a fellowship between a man and a woman who have lived a long time and, one takes it, have an understanding, seemingly unspoken, that they are to care for each other, whoever needs it first. The distance felt in the voice makes it no less sweet, but rather more:

"Monet would never have fences," you said
that early morning in your hospital room
where on the wall
a framed poster showed a master's art.
Waking from who knows what visions
lost in time and space,
perhaps hovered over by shadows and lights,
you must have remembered the Van Gogh
in yet another room,
a small town scene in Normandy
with blues and whites, a minimum of red,
the sky, the parceled buildings and a road,
trees everywhere, of course.

Unconscious sleep, wakeful awareness,
ravelled emotions, loosened fears,
peaceful surrender, stubborn insistence
on staying, on running the race,
on seeing the dawn of still another day.
From the womb to the tomb
we seem to brandish the banner of life.

The rock fence pictured by Van Gogh
is plastic in its harmony
as is the openness Monet displays
throughout his ponds, his flowers
and his slender trees,
all part of the visual sense of a dreamer's eye
and part of the tactile reach of a watcher's grasp.

But for a watcher and dreamer such as you,

whose time seemed to be ebbing
and was wavering between tenure and term,
the recollection of containment
was a thought of death
while the sight of continuity could quicken
the feeling of release from either care.
Chance offered you a gentle sequence
that you might musingly discern
and then conclude
that Monet would never have depicted fences.

"Sic Transit" is a portrait of cool, understated vigilance. The assertion in the opening line triggers a Proustian digression in verse that, in the end, returns to the initial idea; the poem is about coming full-circle. Yet at the same time it portrays a brand of affection particular to mature lovers: tepid, sincere, protective, cerebral, and moonstruck all at once.

The same year he published *Poems to Hazel*, González-Gerth married his longtime friend Tita Valencia, a Mexican pianist, novelist, and historian who, like Betty and Hazel, would inspire more poems. González-Gerth's marriage to Tita has spanned a vibrant period of his career. His retirement from the University of Texas in 2001 was more nominal than actual as is so often the case with academics of emeritus rank; he developed and taught courses for the University's Freshman Seminar Program, maintained his office at the Ransom Center, kept his position as a special consultant to the Center, and published several more collections of poems after giving up full-time teaching. His literary output during these years owes much to Tita and their relationship, for the couple seemingly share all of their intellectual pursuits, tastes, and leanings in both English and Spanish—a luxury González-Gerth had never enjoyed in a lover before.

In 2004, González-Gerth published *The Brandywine in Winter and Other Poems*. Although completed when González-Gerth was in his seventies, the book was inspired by a trip he had taken with his first wife Betty to Chadds Ford, Pennsylvania when he was living in the Northeast in the 1960s. During this vacation, he visited the home of the painter Andrew Wyeth, drove around the area, and took photographs of the countryside that surrounded Brandywine Creek. Many years later, González-Gerth was reminded of the trip when looking at a picture he had taken of the scenery and decided to write about the memory. He wrote the first part of the title poem and published it in *Texas Quarterly* but would later add a second part and compose more poems to join the title poem as the project took the shape of a new book.

Like many of González-Gerth's volumes, *The Brandywine in Winter* has a scrapbook-like quality, repurposing poems from earlier collections by grouping them with new poems to express a new theme. For example, *The Brandywine in Winter* contains a long poem, the aforementioned "The Space of Night," which was written for Hazel when her health was taking a turn for the worse. It was originally composed in English but subsequently translated into Spanish; it first appeared, in English form, in *Poems to Hazel* and then in the Spanish translation in *En busca de las calmas ecuatoriales* (*Looking for the Horse Latitudes*) two years later, in 1996. *Poems to Hazel* also lent "Dance of the White Lady" to *The Brandywine in Winter*, and in its invocation of pastoral imagery and the fairies of Teutonic mythology, the poem is equally germane to the ostensible themes of both collections:

> Such dreadful spite between day and night,
> For definite judgment of our fate,
> Down the ravine to a narrow pass
> Three hundred and fifty years to wait,
> So she can appear and say, "Alas,
> The hands of the clock turn the key to the lock."
>
> A bridge of sighs and a ford of tears,
> Such dreadful spite between day and night,
> Wayfaring souls she stops with her dance
> And wistful spirits with sheer delight
> On Maundy Thursday she holds in trance.
>
> You'd have me dance, my lady love,
> You'd have me dance and sing a tune,
> Such dreadful spite between day and night,
> Longing for respite under the moon

An air of loneliness, an air of blight.
I'll dance with you a spritely jig,
No dance of gloom but a dance of light
Neath lurking eyes in juniper trees,
Such dreadful spite between day and night,
In haunted woodlands where shepherds freeze.

Castles will fall and princes will die
The while we whirl our worries away,
We'll turn to the left, we'll turn to the right,
You dressed in white, I dressed in gray,
Such dreadful spite between day and night.

Come break of dawn, a bright weathercock,
We will have danced to the shore of the sea,
Down cobbled streets of an old Bayeux
Weaving our tale like a tapestry,
Whether it's false or whether it's true,
The hands of the clock turn the key to the lock.

González-Gerth never translated "Dance of the White Lady" into Spanish, and it's easy to see why; the prosody is tightly wrought and intricate. The line, "Such dreadful spite between day and night" is repeated in each of the first five stanzas, and with each repetition the phrase moves down a line until it is gone from the poem. The line itself is composed with two iambic units, each consisting of two metrical feet, linked by an unstressed syllable that turns the word "between" into a pyrrhic hinge ("Such **dread**ful **spite** between **day** and **night**"). This pyrrhic foot is patterned throughout the poem and is the counterpoint of the poem's melody, emphasized in the amphibrachic rhythm of the repeated line, "The **hands** of the **clock** turn the **key** to the **lock**." Moreover, both of these repeated lines are end rhymed in each stanza, thickening the texture of the prosody into a design impossible to recreate or even approximate in translation. The investment in prosody makes it the most English of poems. The Norman source of the imagery notwithstanding, the choice to compose the poem in English fits its subject best. The pastoral, the melancholia, the apparition, the time: all themes and images find their way back to Hazel, for whom the poem was written.

The Brandywine in Winter contains many other poems devoted to women. "The Instinct Within," "Awakening," and "Time to Remember" were all inspired by Betty. "Giovinezza"—which, too, has appeared elsewhere, in Spanish and English—is a poem dedicated to a former University of Texas colleague with whom he shared great affection, even though the relationship never transgressed platonic boundaries. "Life's Dictionary," "James Joyce Corner," and "In Definition" are dedicated to Tita. "Access to Succession" is dedicated to a friend named Gabriella, a scientist, violinist, and poet living in Bologna whom González-Gerth describes as "very sensitive." "The Other Side of the Map" is for María Kodama, Borges's widow and literary executor. "New England" is dedicated to a former student with whom he felt a special bond, and this poem, coupled with "Three Poems for Nena" (contained in this collection) may serve as a literary testimony of their fondness for one another.

Other poems in *The Brandywine in Winter* express a different breed of affection. "Hints of Perfection, Notions of Grace" is dedicated to the late John Frederick Jansen, formerly a professor at the Austin Presbyterian Theological Seminary where González-Gerth audited classes. "Mountbatten" was composed on the occasion of Lord Louis Mountbatten's assassination by the Irish Republican Army in 1979; it ends with the admonition, "The irony of time will not forgive / Their cowardice. And I cry shame, / Their revolution has become a sham."

The Brandywine in Winter also includes "Looking for the Horse Latitudes," written "After the painting 'Rooms by the Sea' by Edward Hopper." The six-stanza poem is part ekphrasis, part speculation, imagining the painting and the perspective within it that regards a royal blue ocean through a surrealist doorway. It opens with the lines:

Something unseen weighs heavy
On the resilience of the mind.
The usual apparitions
Have all been exorcised.
The sea that seemed at first

To hesitate has come
At last into the rooms
Leaving in the dark a wedge of light.

The imagery yields to interrogatives and more philosophical concerns, at first in the second stanza but even more so in the fifth where, González-Gerth has casually mentioned, the lines allude to Goethe (one imagines his *Theory of Colors*):

Could one fall into color
And dissolve in sheer liquidity?
Is space the pure and primal
Ruler of our eyes,
So that no surge can lead
To anywhere but there,
To preordained discovery?

Although this poem appears in *The Brandywine in Winter*, it first appeared in Spanish eight years earlier, in *En busca de las calmas ecuatoriales*. This collection, published by the National Autonomous University of Mexico, contains some poems with dramatic premises. "Tenochtitlan" is dedicated to Andrea Córdova, whom González-Gerth explains was a friend of Tita's and was murdered by her mother's lover in order to claim an inheritance. "Medusa" is dedicated to the memory of his aunt Ella G. de López Méndez—wife of the aforementioned poet Ricardo López Méndez—who, as González-Gerth puts it, "blew her brains out."

En busca de las calmas ecuatoriales was republished in 2007 as *Looking for the Horse Latitudes*. Joe Bratcher, editor of Host Publications in Austin, invited González-Gerth to publish a book of poems in English and Spanish *en face*, and González-Gerth decided on translating *En busca de las calmas ecuatoriales*. Some poems stayed and others were left out (the two poems mentioned above were lost in translation) and González-Gerth is forthright in his assessment of the dual versions of each poem, e.g. he's certain the ode "To Sappho" comes out better in the Spanish.

Like *The Brandywine in Winter*, *Looking for the Horse Latitudes* collects poems from a range of times and places in González-Gerth's career—perhaps more than any other collection he has produced in his sixty-five years as a poet. It feels a bit like an anthology, not quite comprehensive of his entire oeuvre but clearly assigning poems that have been previously collected the charge of representing what he deems more important works. Translation as such becomes the focus of *Looking for the Horse Latitudes.* In his author's note, González-Gerth characterizes the endeavor, arguing that the translation "of a poem is and can be no more than approximation of the original." He then turns to various poems and describes specific factors at play in the process of producing their ambilingual versions. Linguistic provenance is a complicated matter with these poems, since many of the ones in *En busca de las calmas ecuatoriales* were themselves translated from English originals.

Looking for the Horse Latitudes is his most recent book. Sixty years after publishing his first monograph of poetry in his adopted language, González-Gerth was still grappling with the problem of translation: fitting one language into the other so that "the vital nature of individual languages which thrives in literature and especially in poetry, with its particularities of sound and its complexities of meaning, manages to keep its own integrity." In retrospect, and considering González-Gerth's entire oeuvre, it is the role of translation, on the page as well as off, that has shaped his identity and legacy as a poet more than any.

The primary purpose of this volume is to present a selection of Miguel González-Gerth's poems that demonstrates the range of his interests, themes, and styles. The period in which these poems were composed spans the better part of a century so that the collection exhibits an array of topics and forms that connect to different phases of the poet's life as well as to different historical moments and literary traditions. Many are nature poems; many are love poems; many are classical; many are experiments in language. While González-Gerth has produced a diverse oeuvre of poetry over the decades, his overall style tends to lean toward the verse of contemporaries not known for avant-garde aesthetics, such as Thom Gunn, Robert Lowell, Anthony Hecht, Donald Davie, and Wallace Stevens. In short, his poetry is serious and coherent, yet handled as a means to genuine intellectual inquiry; he is Romantic, formal, Imagist, or speculative, depending on the poem.

But the elements that make González-Gerth a truly unique poet are his cultural perspective and his ambilingualism—what he himself calls "the anomaly of my circumstance." As a Mexican who has lived in the United States for many decades, educated in both countries and fluent in English and Spanish, he is a product of this borderland. Nevertheless, his poetry is not a conflation of linguistic hybridity but a confluence of two cultures that preserves the autonomy of each. He does not write in Spanglish; he writes in English and he writes in Spanish. Many of the poems in this collection exist in side-by-side translation, results of his process of rethinking a poem into the other language, but this process is not uniform by any means. One of the joys of this collection is in seeing how González-Gerth applies translation to each particular poem, allowing the poem itself, in its own set of words, connotations, and allusions, to determine the scope and limits of translation: in effect, to recalibrate the tool of translation for each poetic task. As complex as the very idea of translation is, González-Gerth adds to its gamut of possibilities. He has two guiding principles as a translator of poetry: to keep the languages distinct, and to approach the act of reproduction as an art form in itself. In the end, the translation must work on the terms of its own language. It is more important for it to be a successful poem than a faithful copy.

The secondary purpose of this volume is to provide for future generations a suitable record of González-Gerth's achievement as a poet. In the field of contemporary literature written in the Southwestern United States, González-Gerth is one of a kind. It has become commonplace to encounter a Latino author of the borderland who presents his or her writing as a blend of languages and inheritances, posited in a way that claims the culture to be neither interstitial nor fragmented but rather sovereign and sentient and legitimate: *mestizo*, Chicano, postcolonial. It is far rarer to experience a living Latino poet whose writing resides not so much in the borderland but on the frontiers of the borderland, and in equal quantities: in the extremes of Spanish and English and the distinct literary traditions of Anglo-America and Latin America. González-Gerth's poetry purposefully upholds two traditions in their own right, and in this simultaneity he has explored new depths of the vastness of contemporary borderland literature. Rather than participate in the assertion of an emergent language-culture, he has offered a new case of how an author's identity can be rooted in relativism, existing and working with essentially two minds. His faithfulness to inherited verse forms, styles, and tones in Spanish and in English upholds the integrity of these traditions in equivalent proportions, deepening the anomaly of the poet's circumstance. Integrity and preservation are ideals González-Gerth has always held dear. One hopes these pages demonstrate these ideals in his life's work as well.

David A. Colón
Texas Christian University

Editor's Note

Since many of Miguel González-Gerth's poems have been published and republished in different forms, and since this edition reproduces many poems in side-by-side translation, a clear explanation of the organizing procedure of this volume is necessary. The poems in this collection are arranged chronologically: by the date of completion of the English version of the poem (if previously unpublished in a collection) or by the initial appearance of the English version of the poem in a published monograph. *La ausencia infinita / The Infinite Absence* and *Looking for the Horse Latitudes* were both published as ambilingual editions, and thus the corresponding Spanish versions of the English poems of these two collections need no supplemental attribution. The rest of the Spanish versions in this edition are attributed to their initial publication in three Spanish monographs, using the following abbreviations:

VO: *En vísperas de olvido*
BCE: *En busca de las calmas ecuatoriales*
LF: *La lengua fracturada*

The following is a complete list of books and chapbooks of poetry published by Miguel González-Gerth:

Aquarelle: The Calendar in Verse. Mexico City: Editorial Clásica, 1946.
Desert Sequence and Other Poems. Perth: Nonpareil Press, 1956.
The Infinite Absence. Iowa City: The Stone Wall Press, 1964.
En vísperas de olvido. Mexico City: Editorial Cultura, 1967.
La ausencia infinita / The Infinite Absence. Austin: University of Texas, 1984.
Palabras inútiles. Madrid: Taller de Fernández Ciudad, 1988.
The Musicians and Other Poems. Austin: University of Texas, 1991.
Poems to Hazel. Austin: University of Texas, 1994.

En busca de las calmas ecuatoriales. Mexico City: Universidad Nacional Autónoma de México, 1996.

La lengua fracturada. Mexico City: Ediciones Calle de Cerezas, 2003.

Material de lectura, 2003. Mexico City: Universidad Nacional Autónoma de México, 2003.

Nueve musas eróticas (y casi una décima). Mexico City: Ediciones Calle de Cerezas, 2005.

The Brandywine in Winter. Austin: Pollywog Press, 2004.

Looking for the Horse Latitudes. Austin: Host Publications, 2007.

Early Poems
1946-1953

AQUARELLE: THE CALENDAR IN VERSE

Spring
is on the canvas of the Artist...

in the calyx of the flower,
and in the retina of the eye.

Warm on the lap of *Spring*,
Life lives...

The green is felt in the soul
like the green of green eyes;
the sunshine strikes the heart
like a beam of cathode rays.

Reality tempers nothing...

Like a spiral sprung from the equinoctial
point,

Spring has anesthetized the nerve
with perfumes, colors, light;

it has nullified the torture;
it has relieved the sorrow.

The birds trill in choric texture.
The winds caress the dreaming trees.
Warm on the lap of *Spring*,
Life lives...

Quickly, *April* flees with the liquid
murmur of the rivulets.
Slowly, *May* drifts away with the gaseous
cotton of the clouds.

Strange how Time races...
so boisterously... so silently.

June is melting in the sunlight.

Spring
was on the canvas of the Artist...

Spring has gone.

The after-glow of *Spring*
ignites

an incandescent *Summer*,
the after-glow of *Spring*:
the melting *June*,

the brides,
the blossoms, birds, and sunlight.

The solstice marks the start
of summer idylls.

Under a sleeping sky,
in a viscous, fluorescent atmosphere,
ages pass, worlds agonize.

Hidden from the sun,
a naked night sells passion...
Time cannot forget the summer nights—
the reluctant eyes while yielding,
the laughing tears while loving.

The daggers of starlight,

and the tired, shining moon…

July sinks into the vertex
of Life's unit.
August burns itself on the petals
of the rose
like a kiss on glowing velvet lips.
And *September* stands rear-guard
against invasion

by the inevitable.

Through sinuous streets
and torturous alleys,
over languid gardens and tumultuous
souls,

comes *Autumn*,
bearing in one hand
the text of longing.

Season of dry leaves and of dry words—
of anxiety and rain.
Autumn is the time for reminiscing.
But to remember *Autumn*
is to remember too many memories—
all in fragments.

The second equinox evokes
autumnal fever,
a cold fever
that with the rustle of the withered leaves
takes something away from the broken soul.

Love's caress in *Autumn*
is divided,

cut in half by madness;
one half is loving;
the other, frightened
by the epidemic grief
that grey skies shower.

 The skeptic birds
migrate or live in darkness,
diminish life and melody.
The world turns more slowly;
the prayers sound more loudly.

 October is briskly withered
with the treeleaves.
November drowns and falls behind the shadows.

December is lit by the spark of Yuletide.

 Winter
tales cling to the ear.
The solstice clings two days behind the Eve.

 Cold and reticent, the distant moon
scatters light and silence.
Leaning towards the deep sky,
saturated with electric stars, hearts pray.

 The ground is bare.
The ground is snowy. And the day dawns
containing
counted hours,
   counted minutes,
        counted seconds.

Night falls again on dead bodies,
their frozen breasts against the freezing fog.

Winter nights hide
an impenetrable enigma,
impenetrable like the mystery that lies
in green eyes
or in the soul behind them.

The world struggles,
writhes in agony
in *Winter*;
it sings in *Spring*,
loves in *Summer*,
cowers in *Autumn*.
The year is an aquarelle that changes colors.

And as *January* freezes,
February fades,
and *March* awaits the *Spring*,

Life battles on
and awaits another turn of God and Earth.

(1946)

TO SPRING

An Ode

Season of light and soft green renascence,
Child of Diana and Vertumnus born;
Life's day-star that eternally presents
Its youthful spirit to an old world, worn
To near-decay by time, death, hate and war;
Timeless avenger of a timeless grace
Which men ignore who would price all life low;
I challenge them to shatter or debase
The beautiful illusion of your star
Forever brilliant, Spring, oh avatar
Of love, of spirit of youth, eternal glow.

But where is to be found your chrysalis,
Oh Spring? Where blooms the magic of your wings?
You surge forth from the sky, soft as the kiss
Of light, to fall upon and bless all things.
You slowly rise from out the earth and sea,
And cover mountain summits and sea foam
With sleep in wakefulness, the green of hope:
And like the wave returning to its home,
After its journey through the boundless sky,
You are a wave and sleep and cloud, all high
Beyond the feeble grasp of human scope.

Where is the mellow fruit of Autumn's day?
Where, if not nurtured in your warmth of song?
For you bring back to life the breath and clay
That, past oblivion, doubt and death, have long
Inhabited this earth, as if they seek
To render homage for a glad surprise.
You are the spark to which our spirit clings,
The smile we lift to heaven, proud or meek,

The promise that we know will crystallize,
Though you may come and go, and in our eyes,
Leave no more than, in air, leave pilgrim wings.

(1946)

BLUE HOUR

Always this hour
Always the tone of sapphire
The brilliant hue of iris
Mystified with wonder.

Both we and wonder
Never past the touch of color
Never at the brink of fire
Only the flowers
Mystified this hour.

(1947)

ELEGY TO FEDERICO GARCÍA LORCA

Now the larks of your song
lie sleeping. Echoes of darkness
repeat a threnody of sighs. My wings
seek in the night the course of your flight,
through poplars stiff with cold,
under the sleep of the waters,
over the living rocks.

The Lyre soothes the wounded sky.
The Pegasus rides with broken pulse.
Ah, if the angels with yellow voices
and paper plumage could hear!
The air sows death among the ramparts,
intact like the smoke of your voice.
The scream that pierced Granada
is still heard in the stars.

Two misty unicorns
were fencing with their glances.
The cold girls that uncover beds
felt the summer on their eyes.
The moon was your bride, and your wish,
a shipwreck of palms.
Then only your mother knew of grief.

Someone spoke from far away:
only his steps were heard.
Oh, Federico, such want
is that of rabies!
Dogs and more dogs, dogs
on my lips, on the mountain,
and under the bed.
The most nefarious of nights
in which a festering dampness

fecundates black fig trees
with playing cards born wingless.

Even this paper is damned.
I fear it may have come
from tatters which they turned
toward the ground.

Your peace, now infinite: a falcon
of horizons, and mouths full of fishes
because the sea wept so much.
Then the way that even the hair ignites.
All said the silence of your voyage.
I never knew. But today I find
your wish filled with sweet soil,
and a peasant rests on my shoulder,
fatigued and dreaming blood.

What calm deserves your nape
of blind apostol.
Oh, the years and the souls wear shadows.
latitudes turn in directions
opposite the sun.
And your flight, bird and ash
of a miracle, is consummated
in the greenness of your dream.

(1948)

ELEGÍA A FEDERICO GARCÍA LORCA

Ya las alondras de tu canto
yacen dormidas. Ecos de sombra
repiten un andante de suspiros.
Mis alas buscan en la noche
el rumbo de tu fuga, entre ateridos álamos,
bajo el sueño de las aguas,
sobre las piedras vivas.

La lira consuela al cielo herido;
el pegaso cabalga con latidos rotos.
¡Ay, si los ángeles de labios amarillos
y plumaje de papel oyeran!
El aire siembra muerte entre los muros
del llanto, intactos
como el humo de tu voz. Y el grito
que partió a Granada
se escucha aún en las estrellas.

Dos unicornios de bruma
esgrimían con sus miradas. Las muchachas
frías que desnudan lechos
sentían el verano en los ojos.
La luna era tu novia, y tu amor,
un naufragio de palmas. Ahora
tu madre ya te cuenta sus penas.

Alguien habló desde muy lejos;
sólo se oyeron sus pasos.
Ay Federico, qué apuro el de la rabia.
¡Perros y perros, perros en mis manos,
en la sierra y debajo de la cama!
Noche de noches malvadas
en que sollozos de estatuas
fecundan negras higueras
con naipes nacidos sin alas.

Tu paz ya infinita: un halcón
de horizontes, y bocas llenas de peces
porque el mar lloró tanto...
Todos dijeron los silencios de tu viaje.
Yo no lo supe. Pero hoy encuentro
el deseo lleno de tierra dulce,
y un campesino descansa en mi hombro,
fatigado y soñando sangre.

Qué calma merece tu nuca de apóstol ciego.
Ay, los años y las almas visten sombra.
Vírgenes y serafines bordan tu nombre
en el viento ya incoloro. Y tu vuelo,
pájaro y ceniza de milagro,
se consuma en el verde de tu sueño.

(*VO* 52-53)

ALEXANDRINE SONNET

I close my eyes to dreams; I must return the light
Of your reflection to the mirrors of the stars
That fly their luring kites the windward side toward Mars,
And shatter thus the vane, illusion of our night.

To dream now is to reach for incense towering bright
And see myself, fatigued, a hostage behind bars
Of moonlight, which sustain the sky that softly mars
The image of your eyes that now have taken flight.

I close my mind to all the glory that was mine,
The fancy that I wrought from nothing more than gleams
To be a hope, a pain—two elements which shine
Within the light of love—yet ardently redeems
My sinful sentiment. And since I can but pine,
I open wide my heart and close my eyes to dreams.

(1950)

GENTLE AFFIRMATION

Soon, my Love.
What does time matter now?
Soon we shall know the dawn's intention
And the meaning of the water's
Languid gestures.
Soon we shall enjoy the lark's
Pale orchestrations
And feel the whispers of the night
In some secluded garden,
Where each will try to be the first
To touch the other's hand.
Meanwhile we have dreams
To hoodwink our longing.
But soon, my Love, we shall know a reason
For the closing of our eyes.

(1950)

TIERSCHICKSALE

After the painting by Franz Marc

Projected in a shaft of doom
Towards an altiplane of timeful height,
Through fire and rain,
Through darkness-covered light,
From rock to leaf, from unicell to man,
The flight of life
Is a trajectory of force
Which thunders silently, across the infinite, to span
The distances that age the sun
And to transfigure dawn from night.

Embodied in a stream of movement
Turning into change,
Where winds belong to arms
And wings to earth,
Where instinct and revolt collide
In harmony of strange
Celestial hunger, and transcend
Loose matter and its wistful calm,
Consciousness and will converge on mind.

Dark is the veil that trembles with surprise
And peers out death-outliving things
Through blinding light.

Bright is the darkness of the towering skies
That bind the shattered cup which is to sate
The secret wellspring of all kindred kinds,
That gaze at, in the mortal stars,
Their unlike goals and their common fate.

(1953)

DESTINO ANIMAL

A partir del cuadro de Franz Marc

Proyectado en la flecha
de su sino hacia planicies
de altura favorable,
a través de fuego y de tormenta,
a través de luz oscurecida,
de piedra en hoja, de celdilla
en hombre, el vuelo de la vida
es trayectoria de la fuerza
que retumba silenciosa en cruz
de cielo, abraza las distancias
que el sol queman y convierte
noche eterna en breve aurora.

Encarnadas en un río
de movimiento que en cambio
se remansa, donde los vientos
a brazos pertenecen, y alas
a la tierra, donde ya chocan
rebelión e instinto en armonía
de extraña hambre celeste
y trascienden la materia suelta
y su anhelante calma, conciencia
y voluntad convergen en la mente.

Un vuelo oscuro tiembla
de sorpresa y asoma vidas
nuevas por una claridad
que ciega, claro negror
de cielos dominantes
que ciñen el cáliz estrellado
cuya fatalidad es agotar
la fuente de todas las especies,
sombras que ven en cada luz mortal
distintos fines y un destino igual.

(*VO* 69-70)

From *Desert Sequence and Other Poems*

1956

DESERT SEQUENCE

Summer in the Big Bend National Park

I.

The sun descends
in layers of luminous air.
Through the Great Window of Chisos,
flanked by austere profiles,
the distance is resonant and misty.
On the other side of the river,
rises a northwest of sierra:
undulant mountains floating nightward
with the incipient dark of evening.
An ether of silence
burns in the sky, where the gaze
of distracted thoughts is lost.
The sun sets.
And something winglike flutters
amid purple music, as the turnings
of vision and time are deeply sketched
along the languid landscape.

II.

In its azure height
the moon cradles nascent sleep.
Behind its back, Sirius and Procyon
bay in brilliant counterpoint.
Night lulls a slender breeze
with its fragrance of sage:
an extensive night flooding the world,
but at leaden gait.
Oh, how many dead things
are perceived in the air! Echoes
in the wind and transient images.
The nomad redskin, riding the horizon,

anticipates my gaze with his falcon pupils.
...O Prophecy and Destiny! Gods
go up in smoke and other moons expire...
Night is slow
—like the wisdom of Man—; the stillness
so pure, made of shadows and sand;
a bird and its song perceive it, glissando.
Rain falls suddenly, with depth,
terse weeping from passive treetops.

III.

Daybreak...!
Dawn winks behind the Rock of Casa Grande;
nebulous firelight glitters
along the burnished contours.
The sun blooms amid the clouds
and kindles distances to iridescence.
The sorrel mustang of morning
stamps upon hills, races through canyons,
sparks from its hoofs igniting
brush, cacti, sand and stone,
all in the desert silence...

DARK FISHERMAN

The recent seascape flew away,
like a frightened mirror
or a casement that the wind
was never able to portray.
It vanished like a dappled bird
whose instinct spurns affection.

You I remember, slowly intimate
and smiling. But the night
is dexterous like a spider,
and my craft is slightly menaced
by a web of starbeams.

So I have drifted, sails languishing
and net overpowered. Yet,
before the golden fish of dawn
come through the path of purple irises,
perhaps I'll catch your dreaming's wake
beyond the moon's slow-dancing waters.

PESCADOR OSCURO

El paisaje marítimo reciente
voló como un espejo asustadizo,
o como un ventanal que nunca quiso
estar cerrado al viento del oriente.
Se esfumó como un pájaro inconsciente
cuya naturaleza es ser huidizo.
Sólo tu recuerdo me es preciso,
lentamente íntimo y sonriente.
Mas ya la noche, diestra araña, amaga
mi barca con su tul que luz devora.
Y he devalado, velas cual delirios,
mi propia red vencida. Si cuando haga
que los dorados peces de la aurora
surquen senderos por violados lirios,
pescaré de tu sueño la fortuna
más allá de las aguas de la luna.

(*VO* 38)

ANGELUS

The bell of lonely shadows
Will toll in the chapel on the hill
(The chapel of the Cross
Dark by the argent sea)
He who I never was
And no longer hope to be
He who revealed my heart
The flock will by moonlight keep

The bell of lonely shadows
Will toll in the chapel on the hill
And I shall stand alone
Feeling the silence of the trees
While seraphim of smoke
Descend on starry beams
And gather a faded rose
Strewn by the wolfish wind…

ANGELUS

La campana de sombras desoladas
Sonará en la capilla sobre el cerro
(La capilla de la Cruz
Oscura junto al mar de argento)
Aquél que yo nunca fui
Y ya no espero ser jamás
Aquél que reveló mi existir
Bajo la luna el rebaño cuidará

La campana de sombras desoladas
Sonará en la capilla sobre el cerro
Y yo alzaré mi quietud
Y sentiré el arbóreo silencio
Mientras que en rayos de luna
Descienden serafines de incienso
Y recogen la rosa moribunda
Que destrozara el lobo del viento

(*VO* 64)

THE ABACUS OF TIME

An abacus teaches me to grow old
An iridescent memory floods the bottom of my age
And my panoramic eyes dream
Of incapable youths
Of manual numbers
And of sweet beliefs
You ask me: what is this
I shall answer: my hands are burned
Oh I no longer remember what happens
When things are forgotten
Or when the lips yield
To an ephemeral conqueror
But I know that I am very sad
Sad because I am alone
Alone because I am a child
A child whom an abacus teaches to grow old

EL ÁBACO DEL TIEMPO

Un ábaco me enseña a envejecer
Un recuerdo invade el fondo de mi edad
Y sueñan mis ojos
Incapaces juventudes
Números manuales
Y creencias dulces

Me preguntáis: ¿qué significa?
Responderé: tengo quemadas las manos
Ay ya no recuerdo qué pasa
Cuando las cosas se olvidan
O cuando se entregan los labios
A un conquistador efímero

Pero sé que me siento muy triste
Triste porque estoy muy sólo
Solo porque soy un niño
Un niño a quien un ábaco enseña a envejecer

(*VO* 63)

From *La ausencia infinita/*
The Infinite Absence
1964, 1984

THE TECHNIQUE OF BITTERNESS

The beginning of a smile
A stroke of the brush
And a memory of happiness

Why this need of naming absences?

The stump of anguish
Retouches all my sketches

LA TÉCNICA DE LA ARMARGURA

Un comienzo de sonrisa
Un toque de pincel
Y un recuerdo de felicidad

¿Para qué nombrar ausencias?

El esfumino de la angustia
Retoca todos mis esbozos

GLANCES

Sometimes glances
Have a pristine form
Somehow ineffable and frail
Frail like the dawn, colors and wings

Such gentleness
Such grace
Such a waste of words

We should write with our eyes
On nothingness

LAS MIRADAS

A veces las miradas
Tienen forma prístina
Algo inefable y débil
Débil como la aurora, colores y alas

Qué suavidad
Qué gracia
Qué desperdicio de palabras

Deberíamos escribir con nuestros ojos
En la nada

STORY

Told in balconies

The dawn and its glad awakening
The day ripe with iridescent autumn
The courtesan evening and the night of love

Everything happened on the balconies
As did the crystal moonbeams

CUENTO

Dicho en balcones

La aurora y su alegre despertar
El día maduro de otoño tornasol
La tarde cortesana y la noche de amor

Todo pasó en los balcones
Como el claror de la luna

CHAMBER MUSIC

The gravitation of the evening
Has reached the moment
When a sudden chord
Can turn into a glide
The music of a sigh

The piano is now dark

The strings broken by violets

Only the opaqueness of the symphony
Of dusk

MÚSICA DE CÁMARA

La gravitación de la tarde
Ha llegado al punto
En que un acorde súbito
Puede tornar en desliz
Las notas de un suspiro

El piano está ya oscuro

Las cuerdas reventadas por violetas

Sólo la opacidad de la sinfonía
Del crepúsculo

BLINDNESS

My eyes have flown toward the void
And have shed their final gaze
Over the intimate dwellings
Of my dreams

Blind, what will I feel
Now that the crevasses of the night
Have become filled
With indescribable things?

Nocturnal embers will no longer
Follow the path of my fancy
And my heart will behold only
The rainbow of my weeping

CEGUEDAD

Mis pupilas han volado hacia el vacío
Y han desgranado sus últimas miradas
Sobre las íntimas moradas
De mis sueños

Ciego, ¿qué habré de sentir
Ahora que los huecos de la noche
Se han llenado
De indescriptibles cosas?

Las ascuas nocturnas ya no irán
Por las sendas de mi ensueño
Y apenas mi corazón contemplará
El arco iris de mis lágrimas

WINGS OVER THE SUNRISE

Purposely
I kept a penumbra of pain

I looked up at my leveled hands
And from the fingertips like mountain peaks
The sun rose

The lark of life
Offered a trill
And I rooted the hues of my dark soul
In the craving of a sigh

ALAS SOBRE EL ALBA

Adrede
Guardé una penumbra de dolor

Miré mis manos niveladas
Y tras los dedos como picos de montañas
Salió el sol

La alondra de la vida
Ofreció un trino
Y prendí mis matices de alma oscura
En el ansia de un suspiro

YOUR NAME

Your name
Has stayed within my arms
And from afar
From the walls which the vines
Of the horizon scale

I feel the tremor of the sound
That gives breath to its minor symbols

In my arms I feel your name
A tinkling of astonished bells
The drumming of a beckoned heart
A holocaust of passion in full flight

TU NOMBRE

Tu nombre
Se ha quedado entre mis brazos
Y desde lejos
Desde los muros que las hiedras
Del horizonte escalan

Siento el temblor de su sonido
Que da aliento a sus símbolos menores

Entre mis brazos siento tu nombre
Un vibrar de campanillas sorprendidas
El tamboreo de un corazón llamado
Un holocausto de pasión a escape

THE NIGHT WEAVERS

The darkness fastens
With its skillful touch
The circling skirt of the horizon

Surrounded by the gliding shadows
Fluid distances
And the wakes of pinions in descent

The movement of the night
Spins above the sleeping beach
And the moonbeams baste the tulle
That covers the meadows of the sea

LOS TEJEDORES DE LA NOCHE

La oscuridad cerciora
Con su hábil tacto
La falda circular del horizonte

Rodeado de sombras en desliz
Distancias flúidas
Y estelas de alones en descenso

El movimiento de la noche
Gira sobre la playa soñolienta
Y la luna hilvana el tul
Que cubre las llanuras del océano

A DREAM

Something like a rain of glass
Fell over your image

I saw you as in a lagoon
Suspended by clear clouds
Surrounded by light and butterflies

And as you vanished
I wished to give my eyes to the voyage of your shape
Where the sky sailed
Through a thousand routes and among roses

SUEÑO

Algo así como una lluvia de cristales
Cayó sobre tu imagen

Te vi como en una laguna
Suspendida por nubes clarísimas
Rodeada de luz y mariposas

Y cuando te alejaste
Quise dar mis ojos al viaje de tu forma
Donde el cielo navegaba
Por mil rutas y entre rosas

THE INFINTE ABSENCE

Day after always
The impulse to feel myself alone
Alone in the solitude of joy
Far from this company of absences

The absence of your silence
The absence of your eyes
That of the whisper enveloped in your breath
That of your living shadow

I perish in this thirst
That accompanies my anguish
I live dying in this presence
Of your infinite absence

LA AUSENCIA INFINITA

Día tras siempre
El impulso de sentirme solo
Solo en la soledad de la alegría
Lejos de esta compañía de ausencias

La ausencia del silencio tuyo
La ausencia de tus ojos
La del rumor que envuelves en tu aliento
La de tu sombra viva

Me muero en esta sed
Que acompaña mi agonía
Vivo muriendo en la presencia
De tu ausencia infinita

From *The Musicians and Other Poems*
1991

PREGNANT GIRL WITH DOGS

Modestly carrying the secret of the universe,
She walks so casually, a triumph over curse,
Restraining an eagerness so near insistence,
Elated by the sight of a desired existence.
Largely the inward vision from the human side
Converges on the single notion that's her guide.

Now the gravity of her purpose becomes moot
As her step gracefully quickens. Nimble foot,
She herds her collies which, agog their senses,
Assay unseen mysterious essences.
In some strange way the scene is quite discreet,
Vanishing at the sudden corner of the street.

DESTINATION GOTHAM

And rolling with the changing sky,
Gaining in distance what is lost in time,
My train moves fast from afternoon to night.

Through dirty windowpanes I see,
Less and less each waning mile, the land
Just as it loses contact with my sight.

New Jersey fields enveloped by the dark
Give way to lights. The pastoral is past.
    The future is suburbanite.

SOLILOQUY WITH ECHOES

the vast window of morning opens to a solitary world.
before perception lie the manifold investitures
of ageless echoes. and now to act. but wait, first
to reflect upon the sundry happenings of yesterday
and of the day before, this is the proper way, the careful
way: start the day right, they always say. perhaps
if we could hear those words again: how many days?
it will be here tomorrow. do you love me? sir,
we are sorry to inform you...for heaven's sake, let
the cash register ring. or should the church bells ring?
for time is made of money and life is made of time, and
strictly speaking, yes, that's right, life is worth living.

no, let's start again. yes, yes, from scratch.
the window of the morning opens to a lonely world.
before my eyes lie the wakened streets, a modicum of snow,
a small variety of old misshapen cars. get up. it should
be said in exclamation. and now to act. the world
is cruelly waiting though the sun is not yet out. motions,
gestures, all rehearsed before a mirror: to the left, to the right,
up and down, here and there, coming, coming. ready?
for heaven's sake, just why so fast? let's think, let
us reflect. we must have time, we all need time.

so, let's start again. yes, from the top.
my window opens to a world that's all alone. the streets
are practically the same as always. there's not much
difference between today and yesterday or even day before.
get up! what for? it's new year's day in paradise.
the world, the world turns without us. we do have time
to think and to reflect. the ring of money and the ring
of time are alien to us now. perhaps, then, we can hear
those words again: do you love me? yes, i love you. yes,
forever. tomorrow is today. sir, we are sorry to inform
you...no! let's start again. what's that you say? there
is no time? the window of the morning opens to the night.

THE COUNTRY NURSE

Barbed wire fences round the haybarn lots
Retained the semblance of the former toil
Leading toward the farm house, a human foil
At twilight. A window showed disheveled cots,
Prolific as black soil showered in spring,
Where unemployment in late awakening
Compromised industry. And everywhere
The space was dead, dismal the air.
The feeling there was one of hopelessness.
She left the doorway framed in grief.
She smiled and waved, felt like a thief,
Instead of one who has made sorrow less.

IN MEMORIAM: MISS K. W.

"Teacher," I say, sounding like a schoolboy.
"Do I know you?" these words come
From the blackboard, lips holding precariously
A cigarette.
"Yes, you know me. I'm the student
Who once called you teacher, because
That was exactly how I felt about you."

The years went by. Was I indifferent or diffident?
Neither, yet I can't give you reasons for my silence.
You called. I was surprised. We talked.
What did we talk about? About Molière?

And now I come to say the many things
I should have said. For nothing lingers.
Those yellow roses, those roses wither
And fall to pieces through my fingers.

REJOINDERS

I.

Melville: There's mystery in evil.
Cruelty in people is as much a part
Of them as kindness.
Second Speaker: The scripture says,
Thou shalt not bear
False witness 'gainst thy neighbor.
It should have said: nor true,
As long as it holds malice.
Malice is a rope around the soul
Of those whose lips are crass.
Third speaker: Let this cup pass.

II.

Jean Paul: It's strange. You'd think
That men don't actually believe they
Are immortal.
Second Speaker: Should men be killed by law
For killing men?
Such pain seems quite extreme,
And yet there is worse crime.
What if they were to kill a God?
What is this gallows we have built?
Third Speaker: But as thou wilt.

INVOLUTION

I feel you think. What are you think-
ing, eyes thus crucibled in black?
Is it that you have known the link
Of which some claim there is no track?
In Heraclitus's stream we sink,
You in a cage, I on a rack.
You look at me. I look at you,
Gorilla gorilla gorilla.
We show embarrassment, we who
Are between Charybdis and Scylla.

SOLSTITIAL BIRTHDAY CELEBRATION

My mother was born in this month so many years ago.
A woman's body, we all know, is a potential home.
How strange it is for me to have been given birth,
For cells to have found a space in which to grow,
Through the immeasurable mystery of time,
In the darkness of a secret thus revealed
By a loving dream, a dark and dim foreboding
That obeyed an order from an even darker god.

Having survived the nine month shipwreck,
A sailor on the seas of willy-nilly days,
The chain of happenings progressively unwinds.
The most significant events in anybody's life
Are distinct accidents and rituals more or less contrived.
And yet, under the blazing sun of this slumbering June,
I feel, though I draw closer to the day I die,
That my very home was plundered and burned down
Because my mother died, my mother who first harbored
My existence, who told me life was good
And was born in this month so many years ago.

IN QUESTION TO YOUR ANSWER

The narrator in a fiction
By E. M. Forster says:
"Science and the spirit of emulation...
Have made us what we are."
The fiction is a parable, a figure.
(Have you noticed that the word figure
Is itself a dancer?)
Its thrust is most appropriate,
For it happens to explain
The state of man today.
Another illustration is the radical computer,
Which functions as both cure and cancer.
It reads: "Memory has been erased
Of the former inquiry. Please enter a new inquiry."
Such regular, intentional amnesia
Is the next logical step along the way.
It's more convenient to forget the question
Than to seek so impossible an answer.

FIGURES OF EARTH

Vast, restless solitude.
There, the rocking cradle of the sea
Surges in singsong to and fro,
Mingles an ancient substance with the sky.
Here, the sea birds veer and cry
Some bleak communication as they go
Over the sand which gathers now and then around a tree,
Where insects muster quietude.
Fall wind, wind falling on the chilly shore.
Then you saw the earth seesawing out in space
And heard the slow, sure footsteps of a race.
But now of you and me and them there is no more.

TWO PAINTINGS BY FRANZ MARC

I. The Tiger

Hid in himself the tiger lies in wait.
A furtive gauze subdues his piercing eyes,
Confusing them with gentle leaves that bait.
Friend to the wind, an antelope makes gait.
And lightning fuses under passive skies
Two animals in conflict without hate.

II. Deer in the Forest

The early sky arrests the distance.
The balanced blue frames the existence
Of dawning deer. Then quickened by a blow
Of quivering breeze, an ear twitch of the doe
Propels the fawn into a greenward run.
The wood is still, and arrowlight the sun.

DOS CUADROS DE FRANZ MARC

I. Tigre

Escondido en sí mismo el tigre acecha.
Gasa furtiva empaña su mirada
y la confunde con la mansa selva.
Del viento amiga, pasa una gacela.
Un relámpago funde bajo llamas
dos bestias en un cuadro de tragedia.

II. Corzos en un bosque

El cielo nuevo prende la distancia.
El claro azul requiere vigilancia
de corzos que amanecen. Por la yerba
sopla el viento. La oreja de la cierva
impele crías en pistas de arrebol.
Quietud agreste. Flecha viva, el sol.

(*VO* 68)

BLACK ON WHITE

They skip and they hop
They harlequin walk
Looking for something to eat

They dip and they shop
They hardly can squawk
Pecking right under their feet

Just colorless twigs
Make up their wet digs
Nothing about which to crow

There's nothing out there
Nature's cupboard is bare
Poor feisty grackles in snow

ART OF POETRY

For Stanley Burnshaw

Poetry, I once thought, does not respond to human will
And is sublime, divine apocalypse that leads to still
Another mystery: the lamb that on the tiger feeds,
The music played by ancient winds upon ambiguous reeds.

Poetry, I next thought, is merely what the poets do:
To choose and to maneuver words, to weave after they woo
The tawny sounds that spell the darker symbols of the mind,
And so it is the best of poems is the best designed.

Poetry, I then thought, is patterned to escape from time;
Such is the moving reason for the rhythm and the rhyme.
Why else finagle with our prime yet vexing enterprise,
The language that we flex, the hearkened ghost we exorcise?

Poetry, I now think, must be reality's chagrin,
An impunctilious trespass as original as sin.
Poetic art is soft as silk and cutting as a knife
And every poem a tender blow against the chains of life.

LINDBERGH

Not Trismegistus but the god
You now resemble in my mind,
So unhermetic yet so odd:
A scene left fifty years behind.

An ocean, now compressed in time
And space where orbiting machines
Turn the ridiculous sublime,
Painted your portrait in blue-greens.

The great flight overcame balloons.
A journey south good will enhanced.
Blind to Icarian afternoons
I was uniquely circumstanced:

Your Spirit bade me share its deeds,
Aloft the wind charged every bend.
Now it's false memory that leads
Me, like winged Hermes, to my end.

HOROWITZ

His face is austere and yet benign;
His eyes, almost concealed, intent
On distant points of contact
Immediate to the infinite.

Melody will overcome the daily blast
That preys upon the senses;
Harmony, so trivial and abused,
Will now regain resplendency.

Two unimaginable spiders
Have descended suddenly on threads of light.
They run over the keyboard
And spin more than their expected web.
They are the poles
Of the peripherally radiant,
Hard-centered system
Of a diamond become sound,

An unencumbered tryst
Of space and time eliciting
The timeless in the heart of man.

Conversing with those of long ago,
Horowitz plays, at age eighty-three,
And everything else is silence.

SINGERS AND SINNERS

While listening to Bjorling,
Thought like theme crosses angelically
My mind.
The theme is that of music,
But sound turned into thought
Remains earth-bound and has to do
With the material nature of remaining.

Dramatic genres will commingle:
Maria was heard throughout the world,
Lifting our heads with spirit,
Poignant as might be an isle of scorpions.
Leopold, whose profile seemed
That of eternal pilgrim, was once held fast
By one of earth's unusual beauties.
Elvis, poor later rich boy, who changed so much
Around him, more than we really care to know.
Groucho, master of zaniness, music in reverse,
One-of-a-kind gag man, therefore genius.

And so, while listening to Bjorling, who sang
As angels still must sing,
I try to put the sound and sense together,
As we all do.
And wish that I could write my past and future wrongs
Like songs.

MOONSCAPE

In the hollow where sleeping trees
Surround the dark and quiet pool
And southward blow the autumn lees,
Piercing silence the nightbirds rule,
Drawing the distance with sound. And
Over the watchful hill, high strewn
With stars, the skies submerge the land
In the wake of the sleepflying moon.

THE MUSICIANS

Lacing the walls with vibrant strings,
Deliberate cat's cradle of the ear,
Lining the room with wood that sings,
The silence of the trees no longer near,
Their melodies enchant, seduce, bewilder.
Our eyes come shut and language loses thought,
As time becomes a beat and man a builder
Of daydreams given sound and neatly caught
In airy webs of swaying leisure.
They sit and tune the larks of pleasure.

From *Poems to Hazel*
1994

TO HAZEL HARROD RANSOM

because she liked these lines

I opened a book
And pressed in it a rose,
The rose that you gave me
The first time we kissed.

And now in that book
Which was prose
Are two poems,
Your memory and your rose.

SIC TRANSIT

"Monet would never have fences," you said
that early morning in your hospital room
where on the wall
a framed poster showed a master's art.
Waking from who knows what visions
lost in time and space,
perhaps hovered over by shadows and lights,
you must have remembered the Van Gogh
in yet another room,
a small town scene in Normandy
with blues and whites, a minimum of red,
the sky, the parceled buildings and a road,
trees everywhere, of course.

Unconscious sleep, wakeful awareness,
ravelled emotions, loosened fears,
peaceful surrender, stubborn insistence
on staying, on running the race,
on seeing the dawn of still another day.
From the womb to the tomb
we seem to brandish the banner of life.

The rock fence pictured by Van Gogh
is plastic in its harmony
as is the openness Monet displays
throughout his ponds, his flowers
and his slender trees,
all part of the visual sense of a dreamer's eye
and part of the tactile reach of a watcher's grasp.

But for a watcher and dreamer such as you,
whose time seemed to be ebbing
and was wavering between tenure and term,
the recollection of containment
was a thought of death
while the sight of continuity could quicken
the feeling of release from either care.
Chance offered you a gentle sequence
that you might musingly discern
and then conclude
that Monet would never have depicted fences.

THE SPACE OF NIGHT

conticinium aeternitatis
summum raptus est.
—Lucan

. . . night
dwells and I contemplate the sight
that is not seeing, but the light
that is secretly kindled . . .
—A. Crowley

In the shining pupils of a cat
It is believed that all the night is gray.
And yet that is not so:
In that velvet hidden from the light
Lie greens and blues and incredible golds,
Singular in number and circular in sign,
With piercing flecks of violet hue.

Those eyes see life with regular strokes,
Rays like ghosts with differing tones,
Invisible colors no one can catch
As the white of the moon taunts the midnight sky.

By virtue of reflection we all see.
To beauty of refraction we're all blind.
But all things turn to light
For quickness in their life,
Though darkness is by far more soft
In its slow and shadowless retreat.

Light from on high traverses constant chance.
It gives consistency to space
And summons thought from utmost time,
Mixing it all in a continuous snare
That's the survival of a dream.

Ruffled larks sing out their praise,
Mottled glimmers bolting like a precious stone
Daze imagination turned to vision,
Flickering and spinning to deep foliage
Through a gauze of intangible stealth.

In the leopard night, avid in ambush,
After the padded step has stalked its last,
The universe appears intensely still,
Quiet and vibrant with electric force.
A silent and resplendent beast,
It purrs and barely undulates,
Heaving its calm yet vivid breath.

We should imitate such wholesome rest,
Such sheaf of springs so in repose.
We should flee from the sinister gadfly
Buzzing in the boredom of the streets,
And finally hide in revelation
Where only pure liberty exists.

Space! Space! Infinite space inviting
To the touch of fingers needing retrospect:
At the bottom of the sea, the rocky trees;
At the paling altitudes, the locks of fleece.

In what dimensions can we measure space
Without the risk of canon weight?
Boundless or bound, the dazzle of extent
Transcends the uniformity of mind
And the conformity of fantasy annuls.

It is a simple, cornerless beyond
Where death no longer sadly smiles,
Where everything is certain to return,
Even the vectors, victors over light,
Preventing it from levelling creation
Groping in the dark.

Everything moves until it finds its rest,
Everything nests as soon as it has found
The secret ring of days,
A filtering of fateful sparks,
Predictions gathered from the streams of time
And offered to the wake of a seafaring moon,
So dour and pure
That, like a driven conch
Or outrageous wraith in sober flight,
Unleashes a decipherment of codes
Coldly decanted by the threads of stars.

Meanwhile, in the land of those yet living,
The young girls flaunt beguiling limbs,
Their nakedness an incandescent beam
Of fiery, tantalizing flesh.

Let us proceed in silence and disdain
To gardens of indolent relief,
To parks where sunshine does not burn,
Where living makes an eddy and then swells
Finally singing with triumphant voice
Like mermaids who have ultimately traced
The fickleness of sound to triton shells.

In the plummet of a whole abyss
The intermingled hearts of pain
Secretly begin to fall apart,
And a benign existence is unveiled
As it approaches inconspicuous glades
Hovered over by luxuriant shade.
Then solitude dethrones the watershed
Of any wakeful rumination.

Meanwhile, in the land of those yet living,
Acts are all subject to their consequence,
Appearances are what things used to be,
And washed out dreams are still enshrined.

In the nebulous realm of oscillating dark,
Made sentient by some brightly splintered sun,
The zodiac-light can dress in final garb
The horizontal posture of the dead,
Enveloping in passion ages past
And crystallizing marble into shape.

The thicket's leaves continue trembling.
In the gallery of such eternal being,
Pictures and torsos scale the walls.
Landscape is not an image anymore
But land reflecting eyes that would escape.

In the space of this restful, feline night,
While a throbbing void reverberates,
Your eyes and mine will catch the fire
Distilling through the garret of the skies.

Upon the widened, lengthened, layered line,
The last horizon now beyond reprieve,
Unnumbered lamps are overturned.
Reflected fields adhere to blooms.
Close, close your eyes! The blue is all too high!
And playing leapfrog on the Pleiades
The mass of light looks for the dawn.

Ah, but the space of night shines more
Than even that of day.
Every sound, however faint, can be perceived
As if all distance were resolved.
Every hair-raising rap,
Every alerting crepitation
Piercing the air with eager lance
Becomes the convoluted object
Of our wakeful human fright.

The sensory diction of unerring tunes
Allays the warning of the passing clouds.
Beyond, the visible invades the world

In waves that stimulate the skin of time.
Echoes evade the corners of the stars,
Evoking beings possessed of bare
Configurations of recall.
Soft chirps revive the sensibility
Of mold, the prototype of crows
That mark the route of migratory flights
Left tattersall on some forsaken map,
Flights much too high for restful sleep
And much too low to manage dreams
Which no one dared to visualize
A million years ago.

Here, in this leafy growth of green,
Our bodies are transfigured now
And woven into fabric of the infinite
In a conspiracy of geometry and soul.
Because such angles are as swift as wings,
The hand that will caress you then
Will be my happiness condemning wrongs.

In the space of this hospitable night,
In this wooded glen of shaking leaves,
The feverish darlings of desire
Will lose their sway and ruthless thirst.

> Meanwhile, in the land of those yet living,
> A past and perfect reason is adored,
> Wars are compared to simple droughts,
> And honesty gives way to mere façade.

The wheel of hours must be stopped.
We must repeal the barren laws.
We must repel the burgeoning assault
Made by an army hoisting flags of smut.
We must remain concealed as by eclipse
And, tenants of the blue, stroll on the clouds,
Convinced that in this primal state
Lies our conclusive and perpetual hope.

As the duration of the conscious mind
Keeps turning round an aura multiple and vast,
An incandescent register of willful acts,
The fulcrum whence a strike articulates
The luminous precision
Of the clock of light,
The sundog's howling that pervades
The just meridian of the basic day,
Establishing in utter consonance
The hasty reaches of our grasp,
Though causing memories of love to fade.

Like plumes of water, like a fragile rain,
Like the fluttering wish of a caress,
Of a glance, of petals and of words
Is the lover's watching the beloved.
And you will go, noble and unclothed,
On the tide of an unexpected daybreak.
You will leave me anchored in the bay of dawn
Over which you will return in radiant robes.

Neither the scattered scudding waves
Nor the wind of shuttlecocks
Can alter the harmonious strings
Of heaven's harps.
Music can be heard, latent and warm,
The only hum from anguished keys
Able to perform incipient chords
So graceful that they bend the breeze.

A trail of rancour now has disappeared.
Yet rivers vanish only in the sea.
The sea has drowned an echo of mirage,
And we can go no farther. Here we lie
And ask our love to teach all hate to smile.
And from the tops of trees will be proclaimed
The impotence of the redundant world.
The honeycombs will welcome solitude
And, motionless, without a wince of fright,

We'll see each other's arms and fold them.

Meanwhile, in the land of those yet living,
A fleet of promises approaches fast,
Gifts of corruption are indeed abroad
And hideous idols worshipped as sublime.

In this tufted night of ancient space,
The sky will make a prison overthrown,
An open casement set aflame,
A penitence of freedom to our souls.

And yet forever we will surely keep
The reticence and strength that mark our love.
The age of wool, of ivory the age,
The immanence of lamb and mastodon
Roll down a road of molten wax.
And far behind, where everything has passed,
Our eyes at last will slowly close.
A slight, bloodthirsty flame will glow
Within our dear, beheaded time.
Birds larger than the winds,
With beak and talon will dispute
A gnarled, gigantic berthing roost
Left from the tempest-battered trees.
All that and even more will come
Right after us.

Meanwhile, in the land of those yet living,
The waves of chance come crashing down,
Ominous vessels seek new ports
And seabirds flee evils unknown.

In the hollows of the breeze's net
We will not look for our friends.
Life crumbles dolefully throughout,
And there is universal pain.
Must we resign ourselves to hecatomb?
Filth has just spoken the last word.

The trill of birds has slowly died,
While much revered ancestral vows
And immemorial writing slates
Have quietly and humbly become dim.

Should we surrender to the cunning crowd?
We must persist upon the final strands
Of human resolution in the wild.
For there are marvels still to be explored
And that which saves man from himself.
We must achieve an equidistant pose,
At once up close and yet afar.
We must resist the blows of greed
After unnumbered years adrift.
We must recover everything we lost.
Birds will adorn the sparkling wood,
Rocks will enjoy their subterranean homes,
And we will thrive on the angelic points
Of animal yet human thorns.
A griffin's grace will nestle in our breast,
Then ignorant of miseries and crimes.

Meanwhile, in the land of those yet living,
The intellect is under house arrest,
What was a will became a destiny
And hunger colonizes every place.

All those we think that we have known
Now live in some unnoticed town.
Life trickled out through tidy hair,
And ice will finish sculpting them.
As with the motion of all wanderers,
So move the most primordial plants
That model life since it occurred,
Falling to earth, rising to sunlight,
Navigating to ebullient waters
Of millennial night,
Until it deliquesced in the torrential
Flood of time.

Yes, we will rest in perfect sleep,
In this green mansion with its trembling leaves.
In your dark eyes great jewels will converge
From fertile distances and incidental mines.
We will await whatever future holds
In murmurs sent from mangers far above,
Where a terrestrial being was foretold
In tender yet exciting shudderings.
The ravishing demon of delight
Will finally arise within our tears.

Meanwhile, in the land of those yet living,
Threatening vehicles transport platoons,
Strong, weak and rotten mean the same
And rain is nothing but a sport's regret.

Truth is a willow weeping by a lake.
We must not fear the dusky grove
Where voices from the past can still be heard.
Let us assume the path to certain bliss
By entering this thicket's raptured calm.
Let us abandon rueful thoughts at once
As we are welcomed by the tempting mist.

To the frightening scream
That readies the dying
As they hide in the twilight,
Either early or late,
Our spirits are drawn
In astonishing colors,
In shades that defy any semblance of sense.
And the ultimate union
Inherent in silence,
The deep quietude
Pervading the air
Is only the frame in which phantoms appear.
A soul takes its hold,
A remora of time,
Fulfilling a determined

Though now futile bond
That watches past disheveled barns
Housing the ample calendars of life.

In the very instant that precedes the dawn,
As the day breaks out into an icy flood,
Like the dazzling flourish of the rainbow's jack
Everything merges in a crown of light
Like knives.
The glen absorbs us in its nuptial depth,
As the transit of Venus approaches its end.
Everything mingles in a darting strike,
A sudden thrust of transubstantial might.
The wane of the moon is the claw of a cat
Carefully drawn in the space of night.

ESPACIO DE LA NOCHE

conticinium aeternitatis
summum raptus est.
—Lucano

El conticinio casi ya pasando iba…
—Juana de Asbaje

. . . night
dwells and I contemplate the sight
that is not seeing, but the light
that is secretly kindled…
—A. Crowley

En las pupilas de un gato
se piensa que la noche es toda parda.
Mas no es así,
pues en el filtro profundo de esas córneas
anidan innúmeros colores:
verdes, azules, increíbles oros
con tonos de violeta,
y encrespadas alondras que cantan aleluyas,
veteados brillos que saltan como ágatas,
que ruedan mustias a un correr saltando
a través de intangibles tules de sigilo.

En la leoparda noche y su acechanza
el mundo aparece intensamente quieto,
vibrante y quieto como corriente alterna,
como animal callado y relumbrante
que respira con ardiente hálito tranquilo.

Hay que imitar ese descanso intenso.
Hay que escapar del tábano siniestro
que zumba por las calles del hastío,
hay que esconderse y descubrirse apenas
en ignotos sitios del conocimiento.

Espacio. Espacio. Espacio desbordante
y confinado también por tan sombrío,
luz de la luna que despacio invita
dejándonos tocar por el silencio:
en el fondo del mar cruzan escamas,
en las alturas máximas, vellones pálidos.

Todo deambula hasta encontrar su nido.
Todo reposa después de haber hallado
el anillo secreto de los días,
vaso invisible de chispas augurales,
encantamientos luego repetidos
por infinitos labios anteriores,
huestes tardías de frutos desgranados
y ofrecidos al colmillo de la luna,
fugaz espectro de ilusión lunática
que en vértigo astronómico desata
un descifrar de signos escanciados
por la visión opaca de los siglos.

Mientras tanto, en el mundo de los vivos,
las muchachas extiéndense incitantes,
sus desnudeces manan como faros
de radiación solícita y temprana.

Poco a poco,
cual en refugio que firme nos aguarda,
entremos sin tocar las hojas húmedas
que tiemblan en el bosque hospitalario,
incomparable soto opalescente
en que cursaron los puntuales pasos,
el caminar tan lúcido y sonoro
y el atavío volante de los ciegos.
Entremos con singular confianza,
sin resistir los tientos del conjuro,
en el resguardo que mitiga el frío
de los inviernos crueles del espíritu.

Necesitamos una tregua de los tráfagos

que hienden nuestros huesos hasta el fondo.
Entremos en el soto oscurecido,
el soto en que las tersas hojas tiemblan.
Vayamos muy ligera y levemente
a sus desmontes de lánguido extravío,
a sus jardines donde el sol no quema,
donde la vida se dilata y se dispersa
y ríe al fin sobre las puntas de los dedos,
como sirenas que descubren de improviso
el agua y la arena en su camino.

Mientras tanto, en el mundo de los vivos,
los actos no dependen de sus fines,
las apariencias antes eran hechos
que conservan sus antojos desleídos.

En el trasfondo del profundo espacio
se va desmoronando lentamente
el corazón entreverado de los sueños
y se deshila una frágil existencia
hasta llegar a un légamo lejano
en próximos ocasos solitarios.
Y en esa reclusión o errancia mínima
la oscuridad anula las vertientes
que la oquedad anónima despierta.

En el espacio de la noche insomne,
cuando allá afuera reverbera el ocio
y conmociona el eco del vacío,
nuestra visión recogerá las claridades
que bajan del desván del universo.
Entonces beberemos decantado
el vino puro con que se celebran
las bodas milenarias de la dicha.

En el dominio del fulgor cambiante,
sensacionado ya por lascas estelares,
un zodiaco de luz baña en crespones
la materia más densa del sentido,

envuelve luego en su espiral eclíptica
y cristaliza el fuego en sus blasones.

En el oscuro firmamento como viva sombra
se distinguen candiles infinitos,
reflejos que se adhieren a los párpados
asegurando el básico equilibrio.

¡Cierra los ojos! El cielo está tan alto,
y en la porfiada cacería de estrellas
la masa de la luz busca la aurora.

Mas el nocturno espacio es más radiante
que el espacio del día tan alevoso.
En la noche se escuchan los sonidos
como si no existiera la distancia.
Crepitación cualquiera extravagante
perfora el aire con su aguda lanza
y se convierte en parte concurrente
de la conciencia misma que la explaya.

Mientras tanto, en el mundo de los vivos,
se fingen todavía mañanas cálidas,
las guerras se equiparan con sequías
y el crimen más procaz se disimula.

El cuerpo aquí se postra y se relaja,
se enlaza con la geometría seráfica
en que los ángulos se vuelven dulces alas.
Y la mano que entonces te acaricie
será mi canto que niega las falacias.

En ese espacio de noche tan cerrada,
en ese soto de hojas temblorosas
los duendes del amor desenfadados,
los niños de costumbres diáfanas,
se yerguen con sus sueños inclementes
de una hermosa libertad imaginaria.

Hay que parar la rueda de las horas,
hay que cerrar el paso perentorio
al gran ejército de enseñas blancas.
Hay que quedarse quieto entre las sombras,
paseándose entre nubes fugitivas
y presumiendo que en esa casta inopia
yace la verdadera y única esperanza.

En el sosiego de apetencia exhausta,
en el deseo que sabe a incertidumbre,
el más intenso de los tics nerviosos
se adhiere a la imagen de la calma.

Mientras tanto, en el mundo de los vivos,
armadas de promesas se aproximan,
se dan obsequios archipresuntuosos
y se veneran ídolos fortuitos.

Como una pluma de agua, frágil lluvia,
como frescura volandera de caricias,
de miradas, de palabras y de pétalos
es el amor que vela lo que ama,
formando luego un ápice de ensueño.
Y tú lo alcanzarás, desnuda y desdeñosa,
por las mareas oceánicas del alba.
Me buscarás entre las fauces de los lobos
que acechan como un túnel prodigioso
por donde volverás con túnica glaseada.

Ni del atardecer los garabatos
ni los rehiletes del encumbrado mediodía
sabrán acariciar las cuerdas cándidas
de las arpas del cielo.
Se escuchará una música latente,
una musitación de claves angustiadas
que registren acordes incipientes.

Desaparecerá la huella del enojo.
Los ríos ya no se perderán en el océano.

Los mares se ahogarán en su espejismo.
Nos sentaremos en la orilla del crepúsculo,
pues ya no seguiremos adelante,
y apostaremos que nuestro amor
hará reír al odio.

Anunciaremos que las copas de los árboles
rebasan la impaciencia redundante.
La soledad se volverá tan fresca como malva
en nuestras nítidas e inmóviles gargantas.
Y de pronto veremos nuestros brazos
que en cruz silente juntaremos.

Mientras tanto, en el mundo de los vivos,
las olas del azar se precipitan,
navíos espeluznantes buscan puerto
y pájaros se truecan en silencios.

Aquí, en el espacio de la noche híspida,
el cielo es una cárcel derrocada,
una ventana ardida por las llamas,
en abismo doliente en nuestras almas.

Sin embargo, por siempre guardaremos
las ávidas sonrisas y miradas.
Los tiempos del marfil y de la lana,
la duración del fósil y la oveja
transitan sobre cera derretida.
Ya vueltas las espaldas, los ojos cerraremos.
La lumbre quemará tortuosamente
la oscuridad decapitada.
Aves más grandes que los vientos
lucharán por un lugar dónde posarse
en la abrasada y lóbrega enramada.

En los huecos de las redes de la brisa
no buscaremos a nuestros semejantes.
La vida ya se abate lastimera
y lo factible no fomenta lontananza.

¿Habrá qué resignarse a la hecatombe?
¿Tiene el estiércol la última palabra?

Se han ido sujetando los silbidos.
Se han ido adelgazando poco a poco
los vinos del sabor más contundente,
los habituales nexos corporales
y las convexas pizarras arenosas.

Mientras tanto, en el mundo de los vivos,
los ojos se han llenado de sospechas,
la voluntad ahora es el destino
y el hambre coloniza los rincones.

Mas hay aún milagros por ganarse
y lo que salva al hombre de sí mismo.
Hay que mirar las cosas muy de cerca
y de muy lejos simultáneamente,
y resistir el golpe del incendio,
la doble asfixia que viene con el tiempo.

Y sabias como antiguas cabañuelas,
las aves aún adornan la floresta.
Las rocas gozan en sus lechos subterráneos.
Las bestias nutren el aire con sus ojos.
Recobrada cual milagro la inocencia,
habitaremos una espina deliciosa,
punta de tierra nunca dominante,
y un grifo anidará dentro del pecho,
ignorante de miserias y de estupros.

Aquellos que nunca conocimos
se encuentran en aldeas insospechadas.
La vida se coló por sus cabellos
como una luz que arcana los esculpe
y nos ofrece máscaras de escarcha.

Como el andar de todo caminante,
así se mueven plantas primigenias,

modelo de conciencia en sus orígenes,
cayendo hacia la tierra, al sol trepando,
navegando por veladas aguas
de noche milenaria, noche del tiempo,
hasta licuarse en la corriente torrencial
que inunda y anega los relojes.

Sí, descansaremos en sopor perfecto
en la morada verde de hojas trémulas.
A tus ojos vendrán grandes alhajas
de fértiles distancias y minas incidentes.
Esperemos que el futuro nos conceda
el mágico rumor de sus pesebres,
en que se adumbre el devenir telúrico
de alternaciones lentas y seguras.
El demonio embriagante de la dicha
por fin se elevará de nuestras lágrimas.

Mientras tanto, en el mundo de los vivos,
vehículos trasladan pelotones,
débil, podrido y fuerte son lo mismo
y la lluvia es sólo un choque entre las almas.

La verdad es sauce que llora junto a un lago.
No hay que temer del fosco bosquecillo
donde se esconden voces del pasado.
Tomemos la senda de la bienandanza
entrando en este soto de arrobada calma,
y acogidos por la bruma que allí aguarda,
abandonemos todo triste pensamiento.
Ésta es la hora de la risa trágica,
de un suspirar tan hondo como el sueño.

Al aullido espantoso que recoge a los muertos,
que refleja la luz ya temprana o tardía,
se dibuja lo ignoto en enigmas cromáticos,
en tonos que al sentido del hombre desafían.
Y la unión esencial
en que duerme el silencio,

silencio sepulcral
sin lamento ni oído,
la profunda quietud
en que reposa el viento
es el marco invisible
en que se ven los espectros.
Allí se instala el alma
como rémora del tiempo
y cumple una consigna
angustiosa y desvalida,
que mira más allá
de los graneros legendarios
donde se arrumban calendarios
como archivos de la vida.

El instante preciso que anuncia la alborada,
al despertar del alba el álgido derroche,
deslumbrante floreo,
gallardete de proa de la barca tornasol,
todo converge en la corona que deslumbra
cual puñales.

Con honduras nupciales
el soto nos recoge.
Así se consuma el tránsito de Venus.
Todo se junta al fin en repentino golpe,
rayo de sol y luna, apenas el toque.
Un zarpazo certero con fuerza transmutante,
el menguante
es una garra del gato de la noche.

(*BCE* 87-98)

DANCE OF THE WHITE LADY

In Teutonic mythology the White Ladies were a kind of fairy. When the castle of Neuhaus was built, one appeared in 1628 dressed in white with a bunch of keys at her side, and said she was waiting for judgment; on another occasion she announced that it was ten o'clock. In Normandy the White Ladies lurk in ravines, fords, bridges, and other narrow passes, and on Maundy Thursday ask passengers to dance. The most famous is La Dame d'Aprigny, who used to inhabit the site of the present Rue St. Quentin, at Bayeux. (Abridged from Benet's *The Reader's Encyclopedia*, second edition.)

Such dreadful spite between day and night,
For definite judgment of our fate,
Down the ravine to a narrow pass
Three hundred and fifty years to wait,
So she can appear and say, "Alas,
The hands of the clock turn the key to the lock."

A bridge of sighs and a ford of tears,
Such dreadful spite between day and night,
Wayfaring souls she stops with her dance
And wistful spirits with sheer delight
On Maundy Thursday she holds in trance.

You'd have me dance, my lady love,
You'd have me dance and sing a tune,
Such dreadful spite between day and night,
Longing for respite under the moon
An air of loneliness, an air of blight.

I'll dance with you a spritely jig,
No dance of gloom but a dance of light
Neath lurking eyes in juniper trees,
Such dreadful spite between day and night,
In haunted woodlands where shepherds freeze.

Castles will fall and princes will die
The while we whirl our worries away,
We'll turn to the left, we'll turn to the right,

You dressed in white, I dressed in gray,
Such dreadful spite between day and night.

Come break of dawn, a bright weathercock,
We will have danced to the shore of the sea,
Down cobbled streets of an old Bayeux
Weaving our tale like a tapestry,
Whether it's false or whether it's true,
The hands of the clock turn the key to the lock.

From *The Brandywine in Winter and Other Poems* 2004

THE BRANDYWINE IN WINTER

For Andrew Wyeth

I.

Water and ice, the stream unfolds,

Still, moving, moving still, not desolate
And yet alone, open to acceptance, to anything
And anyone whose senses can perceive the miracle
Of continuity, as if all that has ever been
Continues being, such as the bark of trees, the slant
Of fallen twigs, the curve of snowdrifts or the bend

Of boughs, the shape and texture of the ground,
As certain and enduring as the flow of streams
That trickle and expand, the features of the rocks,
Meanderings of cold transparent timelessness,
The slow returning of the Spring, so like a path
Along which nature comes to man, still, moving,

Moving still, not desolate and yet alone,
Compressed by air breathed deep and free,
Long, winding, humble, without care, though
Muffled by the sunshine whispers might be heard,
Echoes that speak of action which belongs
In words, the deeds of men, the stuff of courage,

Something other than the senses can conceive
And therefore needs recalling in this place
Where day and night are simply that and nothing more,
Fair emphases of form, casual delight, the elements
Of chance, before and after history is made
And wilderness prevails, still, moving, moving still…

II.

Still, moving, moving still, as vision
Gives plasticity the meaning of the human eye,
The most refined of sensibilities discerns
The ways in which to subtly symmetrize
Those frozen times half-joining in eclipse,
Displacing absolutely nothing from their cores,

Eliciting profound sensations of reprise
That bring to mind not memories at all
But strange experiences one never really knew,
Inherited perhaps from yet another life,
The gathered stream that flows in dual time,
Events perceived and unperceived, still, moving,

Moving still, not desolate and yet alone,
Forbearing as the earth the changing molds,
Performing all the promises of ancient space
Endowed with fundamental and mysterious calm,
Even such silence as allows the sibilance
Of flights, of subtle wings and waves

That beckon to the ear within the soul,
Appealing to a higher level of regard,
The curious competence to simply apprehend
The secrets which the colors keep as they escape
From Summer into Fall, till circling once again
Winter prevails, and still, yet moving, moving still,

Water and ice, the stream unfolds.

FAMILIAR STRANGER

On this abandoned plot of land once bloomed
An orchard changing only with the seasons,
Plums, almonds, apricots and peaches doomed
To no more springtime for mysterious reasons.

Here smiled in sunny warm and patio-shaded cool
The apprehensive joy of parents' pride,
My brother and my sister coming home from school,
My own desire through innocence espied.

And here I grew first jaded, then chagrined.
Our house collapsed beneath the autumn leaves.
Gray feathers from the nests under the eaves
Were blown away by wild West Texas wind.

Strange yet familiar is this plot that brings
Me memories of cares and careless things.

WILD SURMISE

For Harry Huntt Ransom
and his Humanities Research Center

Horses, wagons, and barns lurk within our days,
A landscape taken from the eyes of pioneers
By scholars able to store up like codices
The prior harvests of innumerable hands,
A fleet of thought ready to sail the main.

Circuitous and strange turn out the ways
Matched by our skill, the will that steers
To press our enterprise with gentle breeze,
Half round the earth to these near desert sands,
Drought that has heard the hush of hurricane.

The antique staple of man's mind allays
The clockwise reading of his future fears.
There too they must discover newer seas,
Here too we must recover older lands,
As once on Darien peak now Texas plain.

ASHES OF THE DEAD

When the sun is going southward in the autumn, and sinking lower and lower in the Arctic sky, the Esquimaux of Iglulik play the game of cat's cradle in order to catch him in the meshes of the string and so prevent his disappearance.
—J. G. Frazer, *The Golden Bough*

When having cried the deeper cry of loneliness
One reappears, such revenant is likely to assume
The aura of a seer. For what he sees
Is not what people speak about, his
Is a narrative which words betray.

What is the purpose of the things we say?

Are the pigeons in the Piazza di San Marco
The same as those around Trafalgar Square?
Somewhere the answer lies and with its truth
Transcends all space so openly confined.
The measure of our love tries to restore
A flesh torn off with iron long ago.
The pious theft must be achieved from time,
Call it a saintly relic, call it what you will,
And celebrate the wonder with the rites of spring,
Refurbished yet, by right of conquest, owned:
The spirit's lust ("We wed thee, oh our sea,
In proof of true and permanent dominion").
The skillful battle must again be fought
Against an enemy in flight but always dangerous
And victory commemorated with a virile stone
("Your country counts on every man doing
His part, thank God I have done mine").

What is the purpose of the things we say?

We say them as a lure, a cat's cradle of sound
To catch the sunlight that will not be caught.
There is no way to really wed the waves or
Win the war, to speak is not reality but art.
Somewhere the whole array of statements falls apart,
A columbarium rendered suddenly agape
Where words, like doves that having nested much too long,
Now break the holy urns and, fluttering, escape.

LIFE'S DICTIONARY

For Preciosa

To be able to say what one is really like,
At least to own what one has really been,
As if one were in fact already dead,
For in some solemn way one actually is:
The final act which is the lure of thought
Being the sumptuous sum of suicide.
And then perhaps a rest, though brief it be,
Before the lengthy, lonely voyage out
Beyond the sea: to really see and then to sigh,
For sighing is a bridge connecting speech and sight.

And so to speak by putting simpler words
In someone else's mouth or even in a book,
To speak while being able to ignore again
Another fact, if such there ever might have been,
That you, he, she or even I have never been unmixed
And feel at least that we are no more telling lies,
That we are holding nothing back that smacks of truth,
That we are never ever never more dissembling,
For everything we said which once was meaningful
Has sprouted not so vibrant wings and slipped away.

THE OTHER SIDE OF THE MAP

For Maria Kodama

The Atlantic was his ocean.
The Mediterranean was his sea.
Other bodies of water:
Lake Leman and the Rhone, the River Plate.
Now, as I look out over the blue Pacific,
Over which he jetted twice,
I think of Borges.
I think of all the words:
Those he said to me and those I could have said.

Like water, the words flow
And, as the winds blow,
They form waves and eddies. They disappear.
Perhaps they lap at the shores of reality
In the bays of time,
Bringing their consummate crests
Of cold illusion
To break upon the heated sand.

Those whitecaps:
You know, Borges,
Those docile little waves, whose foam
Plays with the labyrinths of light,
Seen and unseen light,
Keep returning with the motion of the tide,
Wetting the sunburnt glass
Till it reflects the total roundness of the sky,
The universe that strays
Beyond the reach of mind,
A restless nomad in the realm of space.

A cannon ball two hundred years of age
Still sings its fatal song
As it flew past.
I sit on the deck of a ship

Whose history has been reduced
From the signing of great treaties
To the cruising of ordinary folks.

I stare at the sea. It is a map
Behind which fertile dust has gathered
For my thought to plow as slowly as this prow.
And the blue Pacific
Stares back at me, seemingly
Incredulous of the horizon's rim that lies
Behind my eyes.

There is a gentle sway
That lulls my passions
And yet does not affect the view,
The imprecise configuration
Of the quiet, lush, mysterious islands
Sailing by.
It is all done with mirrors, I am told,
Except that Cain and Abel . . .
Our words are but the quicksilver of stratagems.
Borges, are you there too, as in that other Babel?

EL OTRO LADO DEL MAPA

a María Kodama

El Atlántico era su océano.
El Mediterráneo era su mar.
Otras extensiones de agua:
el Lago de Ginebra, el Ródano,
el Río de la Plata.
Hoy, mientras contemplo el azul Pacífico,
sobre el cual voló dos veces,
pienso en Borges.
Pienso en todas las palabras:
las que me dijo a mí
y las que yo podría haber dicho.

Como el agua, las palabras fluyen
y, cuando sopla el viento,
forman olas, remansos, remolinos. Y desaparecen.
Quizá besen las riberas de la realidad
en las bahías remotas del tiempo,
llevando sus crestas consumadas
de ilusión fría
a romperse sobre la arena cálida.

Esas cabrillas
sabe usted, Borges:
esas pequeñas olas dóciles, cuya espuma
juega con los laberintos de la luz,
la luz vista y no vista,
constantemente vuelven con el vaivén de la marea,
mojando el vidrio requemado
hasta que refleja la redondez del cielo,
el universo que se pierde
más allá de donde alcanza el pensamiento,
nómade inquieto en el espacio infinito.

Una bala de cañón de hace doscientos años
aún silba su canción fatal

al pasar volando.
Estoy sentado en la cubierta de un barco
cuya historia ha sido reducida,
de la firma de tratados importantes
al viaje de comunes y corrientes.

Miro fijamente el mar, un mapa
detrás del cual se ha ido acumulando
un fértil polvo
que mi pensamiento surca
lentamente como una proa.
Y el azul Pacífico
devuelve la mirada, acaso incrédulo
del cerco horizontal
que es el trasfondo de mis ojos.
Siento un suave movimiento
adormeciendo mis pasiones
sin alterar la vista,
la configuración imprecisa
de calladas, exuberantes, misteriosas islas
que navegan a mi lado.

Todo se hace con espejos, se me ha dicho,
salvo que Caín y Abel . . .
Nuestras palabras son como el azogue
de las estratagemas.
Borges, ¿está usted por allí también,
como en esa otra densa y nítida Babel?

(*BCE* 14-16)

LOOKING FOR THE HORSE LATITUDES

After the painting Rooms by the Sea *by Edward Hopper*

Something unseen weighs heavy
On the resilience of the mind.
The usual apparitions
Have all been exorcised.
The sea that seemed at first
To hesitate has come
At last into the rooms
Leaving in the dark a wedge of light.

Is there—somewhere—
A spectral springboard
From which one might jump into the sea
And yet drown in the sky?
Or else fall to the ocean floor
Where unconfessed anxiety
Can find oblivion?

So many things are heard
And yet were never said.
What solitude! What endless prize
Of isolation that is not,
Surprisingly, bereft!
Such silence can be seen.
It begs response and scatters
Glimmers of reflection.

Here lies the tell-tale vacancy
The vacant compass,
The emptiness that lures and cries
With mirror-like precision,
The essence that absorbs all substance,
Inverted vision turned aright
Beyond the compass's deflection.

Could one fall into color
And dissolve in sheer liquidity?
Is space the pure and primal
Ruler of our eyes,
So that no surge can lead
To anywhere but there,
To preordained discovery?

Those people, yes, the crowds
Who are not here, they are so lonely.
They crave the mystery
That can present a future of the past.
They are so lonely, and thus a door
Has been left open quietly
That they and we and all can gaze
Into the sound and some day,
When weary of the walls of time,
Set sail and ride the wind toward the night.

EN BUSCA DE LAS CALMAS ECUATORIALES

A partir del cuadro Rooms by the Sea *de Edward Hopper*

Algo que no se ve preocupa
la elasticidad del pensamiento.
Las apariciones cotidianas
han sido totalmente exorcizadas.
El mar, que parecía al principio
vacilar, al fin ha entrado
en las habitaciones y ha dejado
en lo oscuro un prisma luminoso.

¿Habrá—en alguna parte—
un trampolín fantasma
del cual tirarse al mar mas acabar
ahogándose en el cielo?
¿O de otra suerte descender
al fondo del océano
donde un afán no confesado
pueda hallar el olvido?

Tantas cosas se escuchan
que nunca fueron dichas.
¡Qué soledad! ¡Qué premio inacabable
de aislamiento que, sin embargo,
no implica privación!
Se puede ver ese silencio.
Merece una respuesta
y esparce visos y reflejos.

Aquí se encuentra la vacante delatora,
el axiómetro vacío,
la oquedad que induce y clama
con precisión cual un espejo,
la esencia que resume la sustancia,
la invertida visión ya corregida
y por encima de la brújula desviada.

¿Podríamos caer en el color
y disolvernos en mera liquidez?
¿Es el espacio el puro y primo
gobernante del mirar,
de modo que no hay ímpetu que lleve
a alguna parte más que allí,
descubrimiento y predestinación?

Aquellas gentes, sí, las multitudes
aquí ausentes, hoy están tan solas.
Anhelan el misterio capaz de presentar
lo que sería el futuro de un pasado.
Están tan solas y por consiguiente
una puerta se ha dejado abierta
silenciosamente,
a fin de que ellas y nosotros todos
clavemos la mirada en el sonido
y algún día, cansados ya del paredón
del tiempo, zarpemos con el viento hacia la calma.

(*BCE* 110-112)

GIOVINEZZA

To Anna

I wonder if you are yourself aware
Of a deeply hidden flame.
Where?
Where is the magnet to be found
That can attract fortunate souls
Or the whetstone-sharpened steel
That makes unavoidable glances?
How would you respond
To the brush of the feather
That could be my sigh
In a room darkened by the shutters
Covering an open balcony,
In a country house forgotten by time
If, in a violet twilight I dared to violate
The pact to which you did consent?
Would you set me on fire
Or would it be the same as when you waver,
Knowing the inclination of my mind?
Now you must respond as always
To your lover's meticulous caresses,
Acts to me forbidden as midday to the moon.
You say love with the sincerity and trust
Of a beautiful creature
Who barely knows the edge of mystery,
Of the sharp shudder
Revealed not by experience but by fantasy.
Like a waterfowl gliding
On the crystal surface
Of the next to nothing
That is everyday reality
You leave and return punctually.
You reach the brink and then reject it,
The brink that marks a limit,
The old age that in me waits for you,
Laden with faded hopes

And that, with me no longer here
In a violated twilight
And too late,
One day you certainly will know.

GIOVINEZZA

a Anna

Me pregunto si tú misma estás consciente
de una llama profunda y escondida.
¿Dónde?
¿Dónde hallar el natural imán
que atrae las almas afortunadas
o el esmeril que afila el acero
de las miradas inevitables?
¿Cómo responderías
al roce de una pluma que fuera mi suspiro
en una habitación apenumbrada
por las cortinas que resguardan
el balcón abierto,
en una finca olvidada por el tiempo,
si en un crepúsculo violado yo violara
el pacto de tu consentimiento?
¿Me quemarías
o sería igual que tu vaivén
ante el vuelo de mi pensamiento?
Hoy todavía responderás como antes
a las caricias minuciosas de tu amante,
actos que me están vedados
como a la luna el mediodía.
Dices amor con la sinceridad y la confianza
de una criatura bella,
que conoce apenas la orilla del misterio,
del agudo escalofrío que no revela la experiencia
sino la fantasía.
Como ánade que nada
sobre la superficie cristalina de la casi nada
que es la realidad diaria y ceñida,
te vas y vuelves puntualmente.
Llegas a esa orilla y las rehuyes,
a ese límite
que es la vejez que en mí te aguarda
cargada de ilusiones desleídas

y que, cuando yo ya no esté
en un crepúsculo violado
y demasiado tarde, conocerás un día.

(*BCE* 65-66)

AWAKENING

In Betty's memory

Yesterday flowers were everywhere fragile.
Even the crocuses readied their beauty
Only to waste it on useless remorse.
As I evaded the welcome of strangers,
I feared to discover the heel of Achilles
In everything claiming my love.

If ever I denied you,
I don't deny you now.
Rending the twilight,
A crucifix appears
As lightning in my eyes.

When I was a child,
Perhaps because I was a boy,
Nobody warned me of the danger of daffodils.
And now, as Spring goes about
Replacing browns with joyous greens
And water colors,
I hurry to hide on a neutral estate
When irises and tulips blossom in the sun.

Your hands are alive
In the softness of mosses,
In the sweet life of live oaks,
In the felt dusk of ferns.

Your mouth is a breeze
Now touching the air.
Now kissing that touch,
I imagine your hair
Flowing through subterranean landscapes.

No longer denied,
No longer denying,

We rise like the wind
In columns of granite
And are solid together.

Ages ago the dawn was seen only
As a flash on bashful windowpanes.
We shared so many things,
As time ticked by in our primal impulses
And then flew away with the frightened birds.

My blood and your blood
Shared a flame and a fury.
Your stars and my stars
Nestled deeply in dreams.
My eyes and your eyes
Darkened countless horizons.

The wind chimed its way to the back of the house.
Voices from wildwoods
Urged my youthful wandering.

Wings from distant places
Wandered to your secret song.
We have to concede that life has changed forever,
Like an enormous precipice
Shifted by a grain of sand.
Christ can no longer deny
The Judas of my forgiveness.
Your blood in my blood flows
To the limits of sunsetting shadows
And reaches the birth of my muted tongue.

You stand at the door like a ghost.
Your presence is neither return
Nor the hint of a final departure.
Your fingers casually transcend
The patterns of earthly adventure,
As the splendor of a newborn light
Tempers the surface of eternity.

The essence of being insists on awakening
With battering squalls
At the sea of my sight,
And the dolphins of desire chant
Around a maelstrom beyond time and tide,
While in a cradle of radiance
Everything is drawn into the miracle.

A circular rock has been rolled away.
You have achieved transfiguration.
My heart has been branded by your heart to ashes.
When, as always, the sun has reached its noon,
It will again have crucified the day.
But the early rain
Has already washed its resurrection.
The sound of rain comes from emboldened glass.
The feel of rain is gentle,
Stroking the light of dawn.
And flowers again blossom in their innocence,
Forgetful of the risk in creature ways.

My reverence can taste the ferment
Of a Eucharist abandoned
In the haze of lost and tragic skies,
And I can see with stricken eyes
The fire of creation
As the world is recovered by its glory.

TIME TO REMEMBER

How could we forget
The casualness of sights
Which our contented eyes
Found on that trek
Through woods now ill-defined?

How could we forget
The more than subtle
Rustle of the leaves on branches
Hanging low from elms and oaks
Unconscious of the wind?

And then why did we stop
To gaze at the far end of that field
Bordering the river bank,
A long slow look matching the waves
Of silent water flowing past?

So how could we forget
The sunny satisfying quiet
Of a now distracted afternoon
That later became night
Being enveloped by the dark?

NEW ENGLAND

To Anne

The quality of feeling
Was developed in a scene from Robert Frost,
A modern line,
Words and canvas brought
To the senses that permitted a quiet revolution.

Not everything remained in the landscape,
For some speckles of significance
Were spirited away,
Carried off by chance intruders.

Feelings hide in memories
And memories are savoring
Of other times and places.
They can be wild strawberries
That we picked and pilfered
From fields the property of strangers
Unaware of our momentary presence
In their world,
Where once we actually might have
Made love.

THINKING OF EZRA

Never did meet you
We traded two notes by post
You at St. Elizabeth's
And I at school quite young
Now I have read a good deal of your stuff
And continue to be startled stiff
By the genius behind your frown
Outside your verse so much went on
That on both sides just seems wrong
I guess the world is wide enough
For so many folks to call their home
But the pain in the soul and the pain in the gut
Cannot be assuaged by a song.

TWO FOR STEVENS

I. Wallace Rows in Re-Verse

To this droning on the surf
There will never be an end

With white moonlight
Fill your black hull.

Dissolving are
Sultry moon-monsters.
Foam and cloud are one.

And night blues
Into alabasters
Move outward into heaven.

On the palmy beach
Barque of phosphor
In re-verse.

II. Nuances of a Theme

The place where I play cards alone
Is of constant undulation.

In the middle of the ocean,
On top of a water-wheel,
Or on a lonely beach
The motion must never stop,
Not even the sound of motion,
Such sound must always be renewed,
It simply must go on.

In particular the movement
Of my thinking
Which is discontented

In its repetition.

The place where I play cards alone
Is of constant undulation.

But given my usual game of cards,
Which turn out to be words,
It could be a mere equivocation.

LARKINING

What are days for?
—Philip Larkin, "Days"

What are days and nights for?
Days and nights are where we live and sleep.
They come, they wake us and put us to bed
Time and time again
They are to be happy and sad in:
Where can we live and sleep but days and nights?

Oh, but solving that question
—That hyperhamletian question—
Brings the priest and the doctor and the poet
In their long coats or his paper wings
Running or flying over the fields
Of his dreams.

From *Looking for the Horse Latitudes*
2007

SHIPWRECK

In the fluted air
as from a ravine in which time is petrified
—a coral reef abraded—
one can hear the wail of languid voices,
liquid,
watery,
lunary,
infused with indescribable pain:
voices that become almost soundless
when one does not expect them,
like a pathetic air fluttering with fallen wings
or more precisely fins:
a weeping that resembles the flickering of fish
in their exhausted movement in the deep:
vague fish in useless exploration,
like spies that wish to be denounced:
scattered and invisible fluidity,
slippery,
unseizable,
deliquescent in the now slower, now quicker scripture
made of a shining alphabet,
of a profound and tragic aberration:
a cry that was a song and now a weeping,
that is the death of hope or suicide
once barely uttered in a twilight
or an uncertain yet conspicuous dead of night,
when the moon displays her frigid beauty spots,
when her leaden light falls perpendicular
and surely lulls the tides,
when finally creatures are extinguished
who had thought themselves immortal,
and in their dying found
that the universe dies one star after another:
mermaids who in their final night begin to drown
and are enraptured with shadows of the heavens.

NAUFRAGIO

Por el aire estriado,
como desde una hondonada
en que se petrifica el tiempo
—arrecife de coral desmoronado—
se escucha un ulular de voces lánguidas,
líquidas,
acuáticas,
lunáticas,
infundidas de un dolor indescriptible:
voces que se tornan casi mudas
cuando se oyen desaprensivamente:
aires conmovidos que revuelan con caídas alas
o más preciso es decir que con aletas:
lloros que imitan el ondear de peces
en su transido tránsito profundo:
peces vagos en vano reconocimiento
como espías que desearan delatarse:
diseminados flujos invisibles,
deleznables,
inasibles,
desleídos
en la ora lenta, ora rápida escritura
hecha de un rielante abecedario,
de un insondable y trágico extravío:

un llanto que fue canto y es sollozo,
que es muerte de esperanza o es suicidio
anunciado levemente en un ocaso
y en incierto conticinio perceptible,
cuando la luna luce sus lunares fríos,
cuando su luz plomiza cae a plomo
y ciertamente aquieta las mareas,
cuando por fin se extinguen seres
que antes se creyeron inmortales,
que ya en su moridura presintieron
que el universo muere astro por astro:
sirenas que en su noche última naufragan
y se arroban con las sombras de los cielos.

(*BCE* 45-46)

TO SAPPHO: THREE DREAM-MEMORIES

I needed conversations with the stars
during the summer nights, with the moon,
with the mountains and the rocks,
with the birds and the Aegean trees
in order to find words
that would allow me to express myself
before your chiseled eyes,
your ample forehead of ambiguous love,
your quiet profile,
your disdainful amber lips.

My longing and my apprehension grew.
The magic memory of an interlude
that unconsciously pursued me,
thirsting and dewy like the salt
carried by the waves, led me,
like a map of sanguine vessels
lavish in anxiety and butterflies,
a youthful and daring
Asclepius of the future, to inject
voluptuous colors, scarlet and blue
in avid meditations
which became arrows shot into your bosom.

Swift Artemis,
herding the steeds of dawn,
passed through the dazzling thicket
that clouds the vision of us mortals.
I beheld the flowing shadow
that always follows the divine kinesis.
But my purpose was another: everything
depended on the unaccountable mystery,
the opaque fascination of a noble presumption.
Dreams are confused with expectations.
Memory plays with make-believe.
My eagerness defied the seas and the razed mountains.
Thus years, centuries, millennia

were reborn days and hours, minutes, seconds.
The spinning-top of heaven reached its ecstasy.
Bodies and souls were conjugated
in verbs forever unrepeatable
when the arrows of my thoughts
hit the target of your marble flesh,
the dark substance of your sentiments.

The first memory…
The waters of the little stream
flowed beneath the branches of the quince tree.
The wild roses covered the valley
with their shades, and the foliage
produced an imageless slumber.
The lowland where the horses grazed
was teeming with the growth of clover
and the anise spread
its velvet fragrance.

In an act of agrestic ritual,
the girls who were your pupils
danced in slow rhythm
around an ancient altar,
their dainty feet stepping shyly
on the elysian carpet made of flowers.
And you invoked the ciprine Venus,
offering her some garlands.
We decanted the juice of a whole harvest
and to make the feasting more agreeable,
with your graceful hands
you flavored it with nectar
in the golden cups.

You urged your dearest Dica
to braid her hair with hyacinths,
knowing that the Goddess pays attention
to those who wear wild ornaments
and thus receive the favors from the Graces.
The girl attending you was very beautiful:

her body made of lights and flowers.
I suspected you would not have traded her
for all of Lesbos or the whole of Lydia,
for all the gold that was its king's. And yet
I later learned that there had been a moment,
it was some time before and far then from Cleïs,
when you had been consumed by love for Atthis,
whose passion was Andromeda,
and that Gyrina also abandoned you
in another loneliness like an abyss,
like the Euripian Piraeus. And I came to know
that you longed for the rest that death can bring,
worn out by grief, forgotten and alone,
because Gyrina said to you:
"Sappho, what sorrow have we suffered,
and now I'm going to leave you,"
and you had said to her:
"Go and be happy and think of me.
We loved each other tenderly. Let me remind you
we enjoyed what is most beautiful and sweet."
But you must have already guessed that Eros,
the merger of thighs, would again tempt you:
stealthy, bittersweet, ineluctable.
The sun having set, the night having passed,
the moon with its rosy fingers darkened
the brilliance of innumerable stars
and its own light shone more than ever
on the fields covered with flowers
and on the bitter sea.
Covered with the morning dew the roses
eagerly opened their corollas.
The chervil was delicately blooming
as was the melilot, while in your pain
you wandered, calling in your deepest thoughts
to the lovely Atthis, and your heart,
imprisoned by affliction,
could be clearly heard while beating:
"Come to me! Come to me!"

The second memory…
We descended the steep bluff
until we reached the river bank. There was
an apple grove with altars and offerings of incense.
In the urn there lay Thyma's ashes,
having died before her wedding and transported
to Persephone's dark house.
Before the pyre was lit
each one of her companions had shorn
a lock of her abundant hair
and had lain it on the funeral pile.
In that solemn setting I heard you say:
"You often braided chains of flowers
and hung them from your lovely neck,
thus blending there hundreds of scents.
With a deluge of sweet-smelling myrrh,
a balsam filtered from the royal eyes,
you often anointed your covetable breasts.
On thick soft quills, amid your servants,
you soon will have suppressed your need for friends.
There was no wedding feast
nor one dedicated to our gods,
there were no rustic games we didn't share,
Thima. But threnody
will have a gloomy echo
in the site where we now render homage
to the Muses. It's over. You will be mute and rigid
and no one will remember you nor how you were.
Now no one longs for your arrival
and nevermore will you be feted
with the Pierian roses. Now unrecognized,
you will be thrust to the place where Hades reigns,
and you will wander restless among multitudes
of silent shades. And yet,
from Sardis we still perceive your thoughts
like carrier pigeons.
How we enjoyed our days together.

How Arignota, enchanted by your beauty,
followed you through all the dangers,
yes, as if you were a goddess."
Such was your wonderful prayer
for your cherished friend.

Third memory…
I know that in the dark I heard your voice resound:
"The moon has disappeared, so have the Pleiades.
Half the night has reached its limit.
I lie alone upon my bed. Eros
has destroyed my senses
like a storm that from the mountaintop
descends across the wooded fields.
Immortal Aphrodite, enthroned in splendor,
playful daughter of Father Zeus, I beg you
please do not burden my anxiety
with anguish and dejection.
Come visit me as once you did,
answer my supplication from afar.
Leave your Father's court
and make your carriage ready.
Make haste to come. Royal chaffinches
will guide you through the Earth:
a thousand wings all downward bent
from the ethereal and refulgent sky."
Their flight will be so swift and you, my Lady,
your lips with their eternal smile, will ask
why is it this mad heart desires you
to grant me. And that is why you'll ask:
'Who has offended Sappho,
who has become enamored by Peitho
in the spring-nets of your love?
Whoever flees you will later give you chase,
whoever shuns you will later volunteer,
whoever spurns your passion
tomorrow will surrender want or not.
And I beseech you, oh Goddess, please
to once again soften my sorrow.

Be my ally as you were before
in this war so deep within my heart.'
I still remember all that clearly.
I could have been, though certainly not Cercolas,
your casual husband and father of your daughter
rather that other man you once discovered
seated before the god of appetites,
the one you would have wanted to retain
and could not even know for fear
of his not being equal to the god
who enlivens your visions and your loins.
Before you could confess it, I knew
that you discovered having lit a fire
in me, and yet you could not know
it would have been for you alone.
Before you might have whispered it, I knew it,
though unaware of your infancy in Mytilene,
and unaware of your privileged condition.

Your tongue then trembled with a tender ardor,
making the color of your skin to change
your somber eyes which cannot see me now,
your ears half drowned in surging sounds,
the sweat that seemed to flood your body,
the shudders caused by intermittent fever,
near lunacy for not being able to give love
the way you wished. All that I knew
for having felt and having lived it.
I finally achieved the great adventure,
but it's too late. Suddenly you disappeared.
Your flesh vanished. Its semblance disappeared.
And yet the marvel of your voice can still be heard:
"Oh, virginity, virginity, you have fled from me
and I will be no longer yours...
Those whom I have favored
have done me the most harm...
The beautiful is good, and who is good
will soon be beautiful...
Night gets all back into its fold,

everything the dawn dispersed
with its bright light returns at night:
the lamb, the goat, all creatures
to their mothers do return...
Thus like the shepherds with their heavy feet
trample the hyacinths, the bunches
of burdock are flattened in the fields...
Thus like the pomegranate reddens
up high atop of the pomegranate tree,
up there on the highest branch, forgotten
by the harvesters: not at all forgotten
because they could not reach it...
I think of you only, the beautiful ones,
immutable forever..."

I remember like the taste of that pomegranate
that rushes up my palate,
leaving behind its dreamy fondness
which I fail to recognize in your enigma,
because I find you now turned into stone.
Our idyll lasted as a bolt of lightning
hurled between two phases of the measureless.
Life cannot be in accord with time
when they transcend or just avoid each other.

You didn't throw yourself into the sea
as legend goes.
Legends never tell what really happened.
A storm arose on the convulsive ocean.
Crystals and clamors furrowed the horizon.
And the hesitant space, teeming
with agile neighing
and with languid flowers,
followed its course toward oblivion.

A SAFO: TRES RECUERDOS ONÍRICOS

Fue preciso conversar con las estrellas
en las noches de verano, con la luna,
con las montañas y las piedras,
con las aves y los árboles egeos
para dar con las palabras
que hicieran posible el explicarme
ante tus ojos biselados,
tu amplia frente de cariño ambiguo,
tu perfil callado,
tus labios desdeñosos y ambarinos.

Crecieron mis anhelos y temores.
El mágico recuerdo de un idilio
que inconsciente me buscaba,
sediento y húmedo como las sales
que las olas llevan, me condujo
como un mapa de sanguíneos vasos
afluentes de ansiedad y mariposas,
a inyectar como un Asclepio futurista
de jóvenes audacias, colores desmedidos,
azules y escarlatas en pensamientos ávidos
que fueron dardos disparados a tu pecho.

La veloz Artemisa,
arreando los corceles de la aurora,
pasó por el boscaje deslumbrante
que nubla la visión de los mortales.
Contemplé la sombra fugitiva
que sigue siempre al tránsito divino.
Mas el efecto fue breve
pues mi ilusión era otra: todo estaba
cifrado en el vago misterio, el prodigio
brumoso de una noble osadía.

Los sueños se confunden con las esperanzas.
La memoria juega con las ilusiones.
Mis ansias desafiaron mares y aplanaron montes.

Así fue como los años, siglos y milenios
renacieron días y horas, minutos y segundos.
El trompo de los cielos consumó su éxtasis.
Se conjugaron los cuerpos y las almas
en verbos para siempre irrepetibles
al dar mis pensamientos flechas
en el blanco de tu mármol carne,
en la materia oscura de tus sentimientos.

Primer recuerdo…
Las aguas del pequeño río
corrían bajo las ramas de membrillo.
Las rosas silvestres velaban el valle
con su sombra, y el follaje
engendraba un sueño sin visiones.
La vega en que pastaban los caballos
rebosaba con la floración del trébol
y los capullos de anís desparramaban
una suavísima fragancia.

En un acto de ritual campestre,
las muchachas que eran tus discípulas
bailaban con un ritmo lento
alrededor de un viejo altar.
Sus delicados pies pisaban con asombro
la dulce alfombra hecha de flores.
Y tú invocaste a la ciprina Venus
y le ofrendaste unas guirnaldas.
Escanciamos el jugo de toda una cosecha
y, para amenizar la fiesta,
con tus dedos gráciles lo saturaste
con un néctar en las copas de oro.
A tu querida Dica le recomendaste
que trenzara sus cabellos con jacintos,
sabiendo que la Diosa siempre atiende
a quienes lucen adornos apacibles
y así reciben los favores de las Gracias.
La niña que te acompañaba era muy bella:
su cuerpo hecho de flores y de luces.

Yo sospeché que no la habrías cambiado
por toda Lesbos, por toda Lidia,
por todo el oro de su rey. Y, sin embargo,
supe después que había habido un momento,
hacía ya cierto tiempo y lejos de Cleís,
en que te consumió un gran amor por Atis,
cuya pasión pertenecía a Andrómeda,
y que también Girina te dejó esperando
en otra soledad como un abismo,
como el Euripo Pireo. Y llegué a saber
que entonces añoraste el alivio de la muerte,
deshecha en llanto, sola y olvidada,
puesto que Girina te había dicho
"Safo, qué angustia hemos sufrido,
y ahora te voy a abandonar"
y que tú le habías amonestado
"Anda, sé feliz y piensa en mí.
Nos quisimos tiernamente. Déjame hacerte
recordar que saboreamos lo más bello
y lo más dulce". Mas ya presentirías que Eros,
el fundidor de muslos, te volvería a ofuscar:
furtivo, agridulce, ineludible.
Ya puesto el sol, la noche ya pasada,
la luna con sus rosados dedos oscurecía
los brillos de innúmeras estrellas
y su propia luz brillaba más que nunca
sobre los prados inundados de capullos
y sobre el mar amargo.
Caía el rocío y las rosas abrían
ansiosamente sus corolas.
Reventaba el delicado perifollo
y también el meliloto, mientras que tú
en vaivén deambulabas con tu pena
e invocabas con tus hondos pensamientos
a la hermosa Atis, en tanto que tu corazón,
presa de tu sufrimiento,
se escuchaba claramente en su latido
"¡Ven a mí, ven a mí!"

Segundo recuerdo...
Bajamos la precipitada cuesta
hasta la cuenca de un arroyo. Allí estaba
un manzanar con altares y ofrendas de incienso.
En la urna estaban las cenizas de Tima,
difunta antes de casarse y transportada
a la sombría casa de Perséfone.
Antes de que la pira se encendiera,
cada una de sus compañeras había cortado
una guedeja de su caballera
y después la había puesto sobre el túmulo.
En aquel solemne ambiente te escuché decir
"Cadenas de flores a menudo trenzaste
y las colgaste de tu hermoso cuello:
cientos de aromas allí se mezclaron.
Con un diluvio de fragrante mirra,
bálsamo filtrado de los ojos reales,
frecuentemente ungiste el codiciado busto.
Sobre esteras suaves y tupidas,
rodeada de tus servidoras, pronto
habrás logrado suprimir tu deseo de amigas.
No hubo fiesta protalámica
o dedicada a nuestros dioses,
no hubo juego rústico que no hayamos
compartido, Tima. Pero ahora
ningún treno logrará su eco quejumbroso
en el sitio donde rendimos homenaje
a las Musas. Ya fue, y yacerás muda y rígida,
y nadie se acordará de ti y cómo fuiste.
Ya nadie anhela tu llegada
y jamás serás de nuevo deleitada
por la rosa pieria. Ya sin fama,
arrojada serás al ámbito donde Hades reina,
y vagarás inquieta entre las multitudes
de silentes sombras. Y, sin embargo,
de Sardes una y otra vez nos llegan
tus pensamientos como palomas mensajeras.
Cómo gozamos juntas nuestros días.
Cómo Arignota, embelesada por tu encanto,

te siguió a través de todos los peligros,
sí, como si fueras una diosa".
Tal fue tu rezo fúnebre por tu querida amiga.

Tercer recuerdo...
Sé que en la oscuridad oí vibrar tu voz:
"La luna ha desaparecido, también las Pléyades.
La mitad de la noche ha llegado a su término.
Sobre mi lecho yazgo sola. Eros
ha destrozado mis sentidos
como una tempestad que desde la montaña
desciende a través de la floresta.
Afrodita Inmortal, entronizada en esplendor,
hija traviesa del Padre Zeus, te ruego
por lo que tú más quieras no agobiar
mis ansias con angustia y sufrimiento.
Hazme una visita como antaño,
responde a mi llamado desde lejos.
Deja la morada de tu Padre
y alista tu carruaje deslumbrante.
Apresúrate a venir. Pinzones reales
serán tus guías por esta Tierra:
miles de alas sesgadas hacia abajo
desde el etéreo y refulgente cielo.
Rápido será su vuelo y tú, Señora,
preguntarás, sonrientes tus eternos labios,
qué es lo que hoy nuevamente me aflige,
por qué mi pobre boca te ha invocado,
qué es lo que este loco corazón desea
que le concedas. Por eso tú dirás:
¿quién te ha ofendido, Safo,
a quién ha enmarañado Peito
en las redes de tu amor?
Quien te rehuye luego te perseguirá,
quien te rechaza luego se te ofrecerá,
quien hoy desdeña tu pasión
mañana se te entregará aunque no quiera.
Y yo te pido, oh Diosa,
que otra vez suavices mi tristeza.

Sé mi aliada como antaño
en esta guerra dentro de mi corazón".

Yo recuerdo claramente esos sucesos.
Podría haber sido no por cierto Cércolas,
casual esposo tuyo y padre de tu hija,
sino aquel hombre a quien tú descubriste
sentado frente al dios de la lujuria,
aquel a quien hubieras querido retener
y no pudiste ni siquiera conocer por miedo
a que no fuera suficiente,
a que no fuera igual al dios
que avivaba tus ojos y tus ingles.
Antes que tú lo confesaras, me di cuenta
que suponías haber prendido mis deseos
y, sin embargo, no podías haber sabido
que hubiesen sido para ti tan solamente.
Antes que tú lo susurraras, yo lo supe,
sin percibir tu infancia en Mitilene,
sin sospechar tu condición privilegiada.
Tu lengua se quebraba en tiernos fuegos
que estremecían tu piel tornasolada,
tus ojos grises, incapaces hoy de verme,
tus oídos casi ahogados en oleajes inauditos,
el sudor que parecía inundar tu cuerpo,
los estremecimientos por la fiebre intermitente,
la palidez de yerba seca que sufriste,
casi locura de no poder amar como querías.
Todas esas cosas yo las supe
porque hoy las siento y las he vivido.
Al fin logré el tremendo atrevimiento,
pero ya es tarde. Tan pronto desapareciste.
Despareció tu carne. Sus visos desaparecieron.
Mas tu divina voz prosigue melancólica
"Ay virginidad, virginidad, has huido
de mí y ya no seré tuya jamás...
Aquéllos a quienes he favorecido
me han hecho el mayor daño...
Lo bello es bueno, y quien es bueno

pronto será igualmente bello...
La noche logra que todo vuelva a su redil,
todo lo que la aurora dispersó
con su brillante luz de noche vuelve:
la oveja, la cabra, todas
las criaturas vuelven a sus madres...
Así cual los pastores con sus pesados pies
atropellan los jacintos, los manojos
de púrpura son aplastados en el llano...
Así cual la granada se enrojece
allá muy alto en la copa del granado,
allá en la altura última, olvidada
por los cosecheros: de ningún modo olvidada
porque nunca lograron alcanzarla...
Sólo en vosotras pienso, las hermosas,
inmutables para siempre..."
Te recuerdo como el sabor de esa granada
que huye por mi paladar aliento arriba,
dejando su cariño soñoliento
que luego desconozco en tus secretos,
porque hoy te encuentro convertida en piedra.
Nuestro idilio duró lo que un relámpago
lanzado entre dos fases de lo inconmensurable.
La vida no concuerda con el tiempo
si mutuamente se trascienden y recluyen.
Una tormenta se erigió en el mar convulso.
Se rayó el horizonte de cristales y clamores.
Y el espacio indeciso, ágil de relinchos
y lánguido de flores,
siguió su trayectoria hacia el olvido.

(*BCE* 51-59)

LOVE POEM

I like you when you're quiet...
—Pablo Neruda

I like you when you're speaking.
I like you when you say
all those things I do not know
and everything I never knew.
I like you when you tell
the very truth of things,
when in the air there tremble
a beginning and a gracefulness,
when you elaborate a thought
with the sweetness of a sound
immersed in flavor and intelligence,
when you turn prophetess and scholar.
You enchant me when your voice decants
with your tender knowledge
any casual observation
which for me becomes a song
reaching an inspiration.
You enchant me and disquiet me
if your discourse takes the shape
of an acoustic vision
and a somber quest,
when you question the present and its untimeliness
with cautious and profound lucidity
which is at once a prayer and a conjuring
that in the silence finds its element.
I like your congenial disillusions
from which quite soon the words arise
that musically regain your confidence.
I like your intuition regarding history.
I like your verbal love, your laughter and your weeping.
But I also like you when you're quiet.

POEMA DE AMOR

Me gustas cuando callas…
—Pablo Neruda

Me gustas cuando hablas.
Me gustas cuando dices
todo aquello que no sé
y todo lo que no sabía.
Me gustas cuando explicas
la verdad de las cosas,
cuando en el aire tiemblan
un albor y una gracia,
cuando te desenvuelves
con tu dulzura de sonido inmerso
en una mezcla de sabor e inteligencia,
cuando te vuelves exégeta y sibila.
Me encantas si en tu voz decantas
tu saber enternecido,
la observación casual que para mí
se torna puro canto
que ya despunta en llamamiento.
Me encantas y me inquietas
si tu discurso se pronuncia
cual visión acústica
y búsqueda sombría,
cuando cuestionas el presente y su destiempo
con cautelosa lucidez tan honda
como un conjuro que a la vez es rezo
que en el silencio encuentra su pregunta.
Me gusta tu armonioso desencanto
del que tan pronto surgen las palabras
que son materia musical de la confianza.
Me gusta tu presentimiento de la historia.
Me gustas por tu amor sonoro, risa y llanto.
Pero también me gustas cuando callas.

(*BCE* 126-127)

Recent Poems
2001-2010

THREE POEMS FOR NENA

After thirty-three years

I. New Beginning

Speak to me.
I will embrace your words
without having to reach for flesh.
Could it be that the softness of their sound
is like the softness of your skin?
Once having kissed your lips,
they should now utter only words.
What will their meaning be?
Words have a history
while kisses are the here and now.
Words are all promise.
Even the most exacting are not things,
and never kisses.

Look at me.
I will behold your gaze
without searching for touch.
Could it be that the color of your eyes
is also the candor of your thoughts?
Once having seen your eyes,
they should now see only the light.
What will their vision be?
Glances live in time and space.
They are the kisses for the there and then.
And yet they merge with past and present
and ignore everything else.
Glances and kisses. Light and not darkness.
Speak to me now, but were there yet a time
to come, yes, look at me then.

II. Aspects of Love

Matte and yet soft, a photograph alive.
Muted like a silent song.
I remember you lying beside me,
your head on a pillow of dreams.

Escaping time had been your anxiety
and my obsession,
as if we could have lived in a transparency,
much like water in a crystal vase.

To remember can be self-inflicted pain,
or it can bring about a pleasure-smile
peering out of the gloom of loneliness
in the shallow shadows of the night.

Your head against the pillow
and, emanating from it, your reality,
having vanquished the ghosts of my caresses.
Head topped with light mahogany,
pinned there by the resting shoulders.
Your arms and hands ending in subtle nails.
Round and firm your breasts.
Your waist always promising.
Your legs breaking away from tufted darkness.

Your slumber was doubtless
the calm after the storm,
after the struggle natural to lovers.
Such is the last and fateful image
that I can remember. Day after day,
night after night, year after year,
in one or another sequence
of what is, after all, love after love.

III. Now and Never

The parks were
where we most breathed in the air.
Creeks and swimming holes,
walks through urban woods
close in and on the fringes of the town.

How did we get there, without sufficient time?
How did we get here, without any time at all?

Picnics, meandering conversations,
lying on the grass, or in bed,
an occasional tiff from tumbled emotions,
and of course love. It was all that,
the bittersweet realization of our lives.

I don't really know if the trees or the water
had anything to say about it,
but the flowers and the sun
were always your lips and eyes.

There seems to be a hundred years ago
but here is only yesterday
and today and perhaps tomorrow.
I cannot say I'll wait for you again
because I am too old for that.
Perhaps not being able
is now the only proof I have
of always loving you.

(2001)

THE EDGE OF THINGS

For Rafael Valencia

Something is always left uncertain.
No matter what's been done
in time and space,
twins that hold fast when we think of them.
It happens—and yet it is uncertain also—
that our senses can deceive us.
We begin to feel a tickling
at the bottom of our feet—the basic
posture we acquire without knowing—
and that tickling ushers other feelings
whose source we'll never know.

Some say we should see things the way they are.
But how is it that they are?
Worse still, how will they be
regardless of how they were before?
We should retreat from every conflict
without surrendering,
like cats carefully retreat from other cats,
or like a bullfighter
who turns his back to the fierce beast
and does not turn to thrust the sword
—which might have been a mortal thrust—
but instead walks away alone
through the unbearable ring
and loses himself in the sunshine.

Something is always left behind.
Not in the sandy bull ring
but in the cup of life,
at the bottom of the glass, of the dish,
of the bottle or the jar.

Something is left which can't be seen,
and can't be felt,
and can't be heard,
and can't be thought:
in the incertitude, in the uncertainty
in which relativity takes pleasure,
in the unassuredness that takes possession
of the edge of things.
So there is something left
which no one knows just what it is,
save that it's something that's uncertain.

Truth and beauty,
everything meaningful comes in pairs and couples—
regardless of young Keats's naiveté
are also ultimately relative,
though they aspire to the level of the absolute.
They end up being even less than relative
because they are not at all related,
anymore than the light of day
and the buzzing of bees.

Something is always left uncertain.
After having dreamed of pinnacles
of thought,
we end up in the half light
of the passing moment's insignificance.

(2006)

THE FRACTURED TONGUE

Fractured it is from the moment
it emits the starting sound.
In the middle or in quarters?
Perhaps in the slightest meaning.
It has a need half willful half unconscious
like the acoustic gesture of a tiny hand
wanting to grab a supposed reality.
And then a world opens
which someone ordered anyhow
until it reached the marching end of light
where shadows once again conceal
the clarity of all candid contemplation.
The tongue is left like the remainder of an effort.
It casts about its own deficient lights,
perhaps then and forever segregated.
It wills and can't manage, it tries and can't manage
to make way among everything it feels.
Believing it can think it is deceived and so despairing
it wallows in the promise it was given
by that hand that ordered everything.
It finally goes mad thinking of all that it ignores.
And it speaks while talking to itself.
And it says and says goodbye to all natural means.
Naming things was the first throe.
So many things, so many names, language so diffuse.
And yet the tongue is fractured from the start
between what's said and what's not said.

(2009)

LA LENGUA FRACTURADA

Fracturada está desde que emite el primer sonido.
¿A la mitad, en cuartos?
Quizá en el más mínimo significado.
Existe su necesidad entre inconsciente y volitiva
como ademán acústico de una mano pueril
que quisiera asir una realidad supuesta.
Y entonces se abre un mundo
que alguien ordenó desordenadamente
hasta llegar al fin triunfante de la luz
donde las sombras vuelven a envolver
la claridad de toda cándida mirada.
La lengua queda como remanente de un esfuerzo.
Lanza sus propias luces incapaces,
quizá ya para siempre desmembradas.
Quiere y no logra, trata y no logra
abrir camino entre todo lo que siente.
Cree pensar pero eso engaña y desespera.
Se revuelca en la promesa dada
por aquella mano ordenadora.
Se vuelve loca pensando lo que ignora.
Y habla dialogando a solas.
Y dice y se despide de los medios naturales.
Nombrar las cosas fue el primer espasmo.
Tantas cosas, tantos nombres, idioma tan prolijo.
Y, sin embargo, la lengua fracturada está
entre lo dicho y lo no dicho.

(*LF* 11)

INQUIRY

Why is it that with contemplation as a pretext
I really feel the need
to remain motionless,
barely blinking,
moving my head slightly only now and then
when I see a bird fly by, a passing cloud,
an inadvertent transient?

Why do I breathe so quietly?
Why is it that in an inconsistent way
I try to savor every moment
that I wish to retain being so beautiful
(although perhaps I really would not wish to)
as if it were a torn off section of an amazing fruit,
both ripe and unripe,
moist with nostalgia tasting somewhat bitter,
suggesting a dark prevalence now trimmed in gold?

Why, like the time-measured question
from a soldier on the ramparts
of a Danish castle
who centuries ago inopportunely asks
"Who goes there?" do I utter my own?
Because a why seems always to amount
to a who goes there.
To be, more than to be there, than to exist
requires a reply, a reason,
a reason for being.

It requires less a mediation than an immediacy
as a natural fruit not always sweet
that urgently has such an urgency
and can thus qualify as a sentiment of time,
a life which can be broken in the midst of nothing,

a fracture known though not so recognized
because—why?—we do go on insisting
that we find the asset missing
from an account that is intemporal
and yet successive
to the point of becoming like a clock
and turning endlessly,
for no one knows when it will stop and where.

And I behold the minute-birds,
the hour-clouds and the human-days,
weeks, months, years, maybe centuries,
none of which help me, for they can't help me
even if they wanted to,
for they can't answer the vitally brief,
the reasonably irrational and beguilingly divided question
about the why-who goes there.

(2009)

EN EL INTER(ROGANTE)

¿Por qué será que so pretexto de la contemplación
siento de veras la necesidad
de mantenerme inmóvil,
apenas parpadeando,
moviendo la cabeza levemente sólo de vez en cuando
al ver pasar un pájaro, alguna nube,
algún inadvertido transeúnte?

¿Por qué respiro tan calladamente?
¿Por qué de modo inconsecuente
intento saborear cada momento
que no logro detener por bello
(aunque quizás tampoco lo quisiera)
como si fuera un gajo desgajado de una fruta extraña
a la vez verde y madura,
jugosa de nostalgia con sabor un tanto amargo,
con cierta prevalencia opaca ribeteada de oro?

¿Por qué, cual la efeméride pregunta
de un soldado en las murallas
de un castillo en Dinamarca
quien hace varios siglos dice intempestivamente
"¿Quién vive?" emito la mía propia?
Pues un por qué parece siempre equivaler
a un quién vive.
El ser, más que el estar, que el existir,
requiere una respuesta, una razón,
una razón de ser.

Requiere menos mediación y más inmediación,
cual fruta natural no siempre dulce
que urgentemente siente tal urgencia
que se podría calificar como emoción del tiempo,
la vida que se rompe en medio de una nada,

fractura conocida mas no reconocida
porque—¿por qué?—seguimos insistiendo
en dar con el haber que falta
en una contabilidad intemporal
y, sin embargo, sucesiva
al punto de convertirse en relojera
y de dar vueltas infinitamente,
pues nunca se va a saber dónde ni cuándo para.

Y yo contemplo los pájaros-minutos,
las nubes-horas y los hombres-días,
semanas, meses, años, quizá siglos,
que no me ayudan, no pueden ayudarme
aunque quisieran,
que no pueden contestar la vitalmente breve,
tan razonablemente irracional pregunta
ilusamente dividida
del por qué-quién vive.

(*LF* 13-14)

DEAD LETTER

And if because of so much waiting
I ended up in desperation,
since strangely I'm used to turning in
before one in the morning
when at two
perhaps in a bedroom of my house
I dream the telephone is ringing and I'm called
from the deep bottom of a well
full of firewood and woolen yarn,
of hunger and spiderwebs,
because in the inmost recess of my being
the flames (is that what they are called?)
of nocturnal fires sweetly drowned
the savage scar
of the chess-playing hippopotamus,
of the dancer or the singer
whose eyes still bright
once upon a time vented
the time and genuine climate of my receptivity.

I can no longer rush to write
the remainder of this letter.
I must allow the wager to be lost.
I must cease to write or say, that is to say,
I must desist to copulate and to resort
to written symbols which are crimes of incest
or gestures of a blemished culture.

I must rend away my face,
rend away the mask of shame
and turn on the faucets of the night
until they slowly flood the windows
with a melancholy wind and a timid light,
both fleeting as though tributes,
like the color of the virile orchid,
ophidian flower of such wicked bearings,
crotch from which breaks away
the momentary happiness of life.

(2009)

POSTE RESTANTE

Y si de tanto esperar
llegara a desesperarme,
como extrañamente acostumbro acostarme
antes de la una,
cuando a las dos de la mañana
acaso en una alcoba de mi casa
soñara que suena el teléfono y me llaman
desde el fondo profundo de un pozo
lleno de leña y de estambre,
de hambre y de telarañas,
porque en lo más hondo de mis entrañas
las llamas (¿las llamo?) de los fuegos
pernoctantes dulcemente ahogaron
la cicatriz conmocionada
del hipopótamo ajedrecista,
de la bailarina o la cantante
cuyos ojos todavía brillantes
desfogaron antes
el clima auténtico y veraz de mi nariz…

Ya no podré comunicar corriendo
el resto de esta posta.
Hay que dejar que se pierda la apuesta.
Hay que dejar de escribir o decir, es decir,
hay que desistir de copular y cometer
grafías que son delitos, es decir, incestos
que son gestos de cultura maculada.

Hay que desgarrarse la faz
y el antifaz de la vergüenza
y abrir los grifos de la noche intensa
hasta que poco a poco las ventanas
se lleguen a inundar
de un viento triste y de una suave luz,
deleznables ambos cual tributos
como el color de la testicular orquídea,
ofidia flor de rumbos renegados,
horqueta en que luego se bifurca
la soberana savia de la vida.

(*LF* 15-16)

MEMORANDUM

What was it that I wrote
on that bygone occasion?
The worst thing is that,
if I remembered,
I would not know what it was meant to say.
It's not so much that things can be forgotten
as that they change, that they become transformed.
Time and timelessness conspire and invade a language,
depriving it of sense
and end up transposing the edge,
which was in some way real,
of a living tongue which is now awkward,
a dereliction, a masquerade dancing
the dance of the Lilliputians.

Woe is me, might say the desert denizen,
whose words only the wind, the sun and the sand can hear.
I hereby denounce—and don't announce—
everything said yesterday, today and tomorrow,
on the edge of plotting a delinquency
that dawns on the line of the horizon
only to fall in the night of the abyss
that is the last and lasting memory.

(2009)

MEMORIAL

¿Qué fue lo que escribí
en aquella coyuntura de ocasión?
Lo peor es que si lo hallara
ya no sabría lo que quería decir.
No es tanto que las cosas se olviden
como que se transforman.
El tiempo y la ucronía
se confabulan invadiendo
y quitándole sentido a los vocablos,
para acabar, sí, trastocando
el filo que fue real de alguna forma,
de alguna lengua viva
y que ahora es sólo una torpeza,
un desvalimiento,
una mascarada que baila el baile
de los liliputienses.

Guay de mí, diría el hombre del desierto,
cuyas palabras no las oyen
más que el viento, el sol, la arena.
Yo aquí denuncio—y no enuncio—
todo lo dicho ayer, hoy y mañana,
al borde del esquema de un delito
que amanece en la línea horizontal para caer
luego en la noche del abismo
que es, al fin y al cabo, el único recuerdo.

(*LF* 19)

WORDS AND QUESTIONS

And now abideth faith, hope, love...
But the greatest of these is love.
— 1 Corinthians 13

Can we actually suppose that we communicate that which we say,
that what we say someone else can understand,
and that, in turn, the other can communicate that which he says,
so that in consequence what the other says we understand?
Is communication possible at last?
To what degree?
At what level can meaning be transferred?

An idea is always partially concealed
no matter to what end you try to make it clear.
Idea is precisely the opposite of thing;
that is to say it's something that is far from being
something one can hand over to someone.
But words are felt to be mediators of ideas,
a vague expression of wishing to commune,
a vehicle of touch nonetheless uncertain
reaching a point next to what it signifies,
which corresponds—without responding—to a lump of sugar
which enjoys making love as it dissolves
in the apostolic and gradual palate of the mind
until achieving the corresponding form of sound.

How to separate what's said from what's not said?
Where can we find the true essence of the sign?
For nonetheless, bitterly and happily, for instance:
love is not a word when its meaning has been found.

(2009)

PALABRAS Y PREGUNTAS

Y ahora permanecen la fe, la esperanza, y el amor...
Empero, el mayor de éstos es el amor.
— 1 Corintios 13

¿Acaso cabe suponer que uno comunica lo que dice,
que lo que uno dice otro lo entiende,
que, a su vez, ese otro comunica lo que dice,
que, en consecuencia, lo que dice aquél uno lo entiende?
¿Será por fin la comunicación posible?
¿Hasta qué grado?
¿En qué nivel existe la transferencia de sentidos?

Velada un tanto siempre está la idea
que se devela menos cuanto más se la desvela.
La idea es precisamente lo opuesto de la cosa;
es decir, es una cosa de por sí muy lejos
de ser cosa que puede darse incluso con la mano.
Mas la palabra se siente mediadora de la idea,
vaga expresión del comulgar querido,
vehículo de un tacto al fin y al cabo incierto
que alcanza un punto próximo a lo que significa,
que corresponde—y no responde—a un terrón de azúcar
que goza enamorando según se va desmoronando
en el paulino y paulatino paladar del pensamiento
hasta lograr la forma consecuente del sonido.

¿Cómo apartar lo dicho y lo no dicho?
¿Dónde radica el carácter singular del signo?
Pues, sin embargo, amarga y felizmente, por ejemplo:
amor ya no es palabra al disolverse en su sentido.

(*LF* 25-26)

THE WRITTEN WORD

After reading Rilke's text
entitled "Urgeräusch"

Where might I have written the lines
which now make up this poem?
At what juncture of time and space
—conundrum of experiences made up—
wrote I what seems that I say here?
Because I'm sure that in the marrow
of these sounding and spelled bones
it has been written by someone like myself
—if not by me—
who thinks my name is such and so
and who is called just as I call myself.
And what if this had only been thought up?
That does not matter.
To think is to write as it is written
in the frontal suture of the skull,
perhaps also in the creases of the brain
like folds of paper
wet with salt from ancient tree-like seas
such as the corals living in their depths.
To speculate is to reflect what has been written
in those grooves reached barely by the wind,
erasing everything it can erase, even what seems
to be more indelible than silence.
That reflection is then thought and later written
in gray ink by ideas resembling tentacles
which are the insubstantiality of our feelings.

Everything is written except what can't be written.
And yet what has been written is suddenly erased
by currents of rivers, transparent like glass,
ageless nurture turned into fisher's nets.

What I have written here, if I have written right,
will also not remain.
Fishing is artful
and barely a magic trick using hands and sleeves.
From every line remains hardly a thing
of what at one time swam, of what at one time passed
in the waters of some consciousness.

But then I don't recall
what I believe I either phrased or paraphrased.
Could it be that the needle of the mental phonograph
stopped plowing the furrows of the brain,
preventing all ability to write
and making all wise and eager words
to lose their verity?

(2009)

ESCRITURA

Inspirado en el texto Urgeräusch
de Rainer Maria Rilke

¿Dónde habré escrito los versos
que ahora aparecen en este poema?
¿En qué coyuntura de tiempo y espacio
—acertijo de experiencias inventadas—
escribí ya lo que parece que aquí digo?
Porque estoy seguro de que el tuétano
de estos huesos sonoros o alfabéticos
ya ha sido escrito por alguien como yo
—si no por mí—
que creo que soy y que me llamo tal
y que me llaman tal como me llamo.
¿Y si esto hubiera sido pensado solamente?
Eso no importa.
Pensar es escribir como está inscrito
en la sutura coronal del cráneo,
quizá también entre los pliegues del cerebro
que son dobleces de un papel
mojado por la sal de un viejo mar arbóreo
como el coral que habita en sus profundidades.
Especular es reflejar lo que está escrito
en esa especie de ranuras donde apenas llega el viento
que borra todo lo borrable, hasta lo que parece
ser más indeleble que el silencio.
Ese reflejo que después se piensa después se escribe
con la tinta gris que los tentáculos de las ideas
simulan, siendo la insustancia de nuestros sentimientos.

Todo está escrito salvo lo que no se escribe.
Y está suscrito lo que ciertamente tiene estilo
de cálamos y plumas. De lejos hasta aquí
lo que parece escrito se borra de repente

en la corriente de los ríos, visos de vidrio,
alimento milenario y luego redes pescadoras.
Lo que yo he escrito aquí, si bien lo he escrito,
tampoco va a quedarse. La pesca es engañosa
y apenas suerte mágica de manos y de mangas.
De cada verso queda ni siquiera nada
de lo que a veces nada, de lo que a veces
pasa por las aguas de la circunstancia.
Y luego tampoco ya me acuerdo
de lo que creo haber fraseado o parafraseado.

¿Será que la dichosa aguja del fonógrafo mental
dejó de arar los surcos del encéfalo
y que la habilidad de la revelación se hizo ágrafa,
dejando a las palabras ávidas y sabias
que perdieran su constancia?

(*LF* 27-28)

SECOND THOUGHT

I thought of it again.

It might have been my fascination with the light
that came in through the window,
whose rays, almost invisible, were
like cobwebs torn to shreds
or like splinters of gold in the breeze.
How strange it was that at that very hour,
which should have been precise
and yet was not, instead there was a sound
that fell against the wall opposite me.
And while the light was sounding lightly,
my eyes searched for the sense
which might explain such province,
such place which seemed to have been sent
by heaven as one imagines it
and which in fact could be a revelation.
And yet everything seemed to advance
in a way which was inevitable
and, of course, without a flaw,
as if what is supposed as individual
becomes dissolved in the generic.
No doubt there lay the secret.

I thought of it again.

(2009)

SECRETS

Could it be that
we have reached the point of saying nothing that's coherent?
Or grammatical sometimes?
You pictures paint,
paint pictures I,
what is the difference in the final count?
No logical sense to threading words
like not being able to pass the eye through a needle
without leaving a trace of capricious blue
or capriciously strip off the eye of a branch
in the waters of a murky and thirsting moon.

Could the time have come for inevitable silence,
killing desires to communicate, leaving the mind to flounder
though it persists like a caged bird,
fluttering without a course?
Such is the mind when possessed by that which can't
be named because there are no words to describe it
and there is no breath to barely sketch it.
The tongue has been cut, has been fractured,
a limit is reached, the courage of the soul erased
and, babbling, it shifts dots over the eyes
with ellipsis marks and you laugh because you think
    you know the secret
of the incommunication which afflicts us.

Sometimes I'm surprised by the shadow of the sun
through the leaves of a flimsy eucalyptus,
bent like a man as old as Adam.
I say root instead of tree
and stone instead of clay.
And you say fire instead of ice.
And I seek God and find the Devil.
Innocent errors, not mistakes

but signs of visions being friendly
yet turned out—so they tell me—quite unhappy.

There are secrets like a puzzle or the riddle
   of the Sphinx
which Oedipus was able to decipher,
though after vanquishing the monster
he was blinded by tides beyond his power.
But there are others more profound and deep
which are called mysteries
and which cannot be separated
from their clusters of ubiquity,
mysteries which where not known
even to Pharaohs,
mysteries barely heard as notes as vague as twilight.
Is this prose I'm writing?

And so it's only music that explains
the being and the feeling of the living.
Yet I cannot, no, you cannot manage to explain,
for we're not able even to express exactly
what that assertion means,
it doesn't fit within the syllables
remaining in my barren beehive,
A B C D,
A E I O no longer fit
in our miserable Pandora's box.

We lose our lives because we lose our days.
And what are days?
You tell me that they measure time,
points of information, of our relations,
winking of gods we never see.
What is time outside the clock?
A speck in the eye that longs for the taste
of mint no longer on the tongue,
the tongue that is and will remain fragmented,
that has become and will forever be a dark night
without—inevitably—stars.

(2010)

SECRETOS

¿Será que
hemos llegado al punto de no poder decir ya nada
    coherente?
¿Ni gramatical a veces?
Pinto cuadros yo,
pintas tú cuadros.
De no poder hilar palabras con sentido lógico,
como aquello
de no poder pasar el ojo por la aguja
sin dejar un trazo de azul vertiginoso,
o vertiginosamente deshojar el ojo de una rama
en el agua de una luna lóbrega y sedienta.

¿Habrá llegado la hora del silencio
que aniquila los deseos comunicantes
como vasos de un ayer menospreciado,
dejando el pensamiento aniquilado
aunque persiste como pájaro ululante,
aleteando pero ya sin ruta?
Tal es el pensamiento cuando surge aquello
que no se puede definir porque faltan los vocablos
y faltaría el aliento para apenas esbozarlos.
La lengua se ha truncado, fracturado, se ha llegado
a un límite y obliterado queda el ánimo del ánima
que ahora balbuceante tergiversa los puntos de las íes
con los puntos suspensivos, y te ríes porque crees
    que sabes el secreto
de la incomunicación que nos aflige.

A veces me sorprende la sombra de aquel sol
entre las hojas de un eufórbico eucalipto
hoy ralo y encorvado como un viejo.
Dices raíz en vez de árbol,
igual que piedra en vez de barro.

Yo a veces digo fuego en vez de hielo,
y busco a Dios y encuentro al Diablo.
Errores inocentes, no equivocaciones
sino señales de visiones que quieren ser amables
pero resultan—nos dicen—desafortunadas.

Secretos hay como la adivinanza o acertijo de la Esfinge
que por su inteligencia Edipo pudo descifrar,
aunque venciendo al monstruo quedó ciego
por circunstancias posteriores más allá de su poder.
Pero hay otros más profundos y más hondos,
más confusos llamándose misterios
los cuales no se logra desprender
de sus racimos en la ubicuidad,
misterios que nunca fueron conocidos ni de los faraones,
misterios apenas escuchados como notas vagas
    y crepusculares.
¿Son acaso prosaísmos lo que escribo?

Y entonces es la música
que explica el ser y el sentir de los vivientes.
Mas yo no puedo y tú no puedes alcanzar ese explicar,
pues ni siquiera podemos expresar debidamente
lo que digo, lo que tú quieres decir,
no se comprende en las sílabas
que permanecen en las casillas de mi panal de abejas,
a be ce de,
A E I O no, no caben ya
en la caja de nuestra mísera Pandora.

Se nos va la vida porque se nos van los días.
¿Qué son los días?
Me dices que son medidas en el tiempo,
puntos de razón, de relación,
parpadeos de dioses que nunca se verán.
¿Qué es el tiempo fuera del reloj?

Una maraña que lamenta
el sabor de aquella menta que ya no hay
  sobre la lengua,
la lengua que queda fracturada
en que ha caído una noche oscura
sin—inevitablemente—estrellas.

TABULA RASA

The other day it happened
that tomorrow became yesterday.
It felt like a surprise,
like an omen of something that would go on happening.
Suddenly I realized that the tale,
that old fairy tale
they told me, wasn't true.
Yes, that simple fairy tale
of when I was a still a child and enjoyed
life without knowing what time was.
Today I wish I could manage for my poems
the roundness they say the world has,
the world that turns like the hands of the clock
not knowing when the winding will wind down.
Although there's no more winding
for it's an electric current
that runs and then goes step by step
marking the seconds of intransferable grief,
turning yesterday into tomorrow,
today serving no purpose,
until you reach the place where winds don't blow,
where the sun doesn't shine,
where the rain doesn't fall
and the trees are all downcast,
with no reason for being but the warmth that comes in
through Winter's window, it comes remembering
what we believed in days gone by,
that old fairy tale which turns out true,
those days without afternoon or night
when tomorrow became yesterday.

(2010)

TABULA RASA

El otro día ocurrió
que mañana se convirtió en ayer.
Lo sentí como sorpresa,
como un anuncio de eso que iba a seguir pasando.
De pronto caí en la cuenta de que el cuento,
aquel viejo cuento de hadas
que me habían contado, no era cierto.
Sí, aquel simple cuento de hadas
de cuando yo era todavía pequeño y gozaba
de la vida sin saber lo que era el tiempo.
Hoy quisiera procurar para mis versos
la redondez que dicen tiene el mundo,
el mundo que da vueltas como las manecillas del reloj
sin saber cuándo se acabará la cuerda.
Aunque ya tampoco hay cuerda
pues es una corriente eléctrica
que corre pero se convierte en un ir paso a paso
que marca los segundos de un duelo intransferible,
convirtiendo el ayer en el mañana.
Pues de nada sirve el hoy,
hasta llegar a la región en que el viento ya no sopla,
en que el sol ya no brilla,
en que la lluvia ya no cae
y los árboles se encuentran cabizbajos,
sin razón de ser pero con el calor que entra
por la ventana del invierno y va rememorando
lo que creímos otro día,
el viejo cuento de hadas que acaba siendo cierto,
aquel día sin tarde o noche
cuando el mañana se convirtió en ayer.

Interview with Miguel González-Gerth

DAC: I usually hesitate before asking a poet or an author in any genre about influence, literary influence, because sometimes it can feel contrived, like putting the cart before the horse, or superficial. But in reading your poetry, and particularly looking at the various forms and voices that your poems have, it seems that influence is very great in your work. So let's begin with the question: At different stages of your writing career, who were you reading, and to what extent did you feel influenced?

MGG: What filtered through?

DAC: Precisely.

MGG: Well, I think we have to do this in a way chronologically, to apply chronology to the biography and the literary consequences. As you know, I was born in Mexico City and started my schooling there. That's before I could really detect that there was anything particular about literature that would eventually come to be one of the most important things in my life. An uncle of mine—uncle by marriage, he married an aunt of mine, a sister of my mother's—was a poet. And I suppose he was the first sort of model—not so much that I was already doing any writing to the point that he would be an influence in the writing—but an influence simply in the fact that he was a poet. He wrote poetry that was in a way lyrical and yet had an epic tonality. He wrote a poem that became very famous in Mexico, called *Credo*. And it was an invocation of Mexico itself. He wrote it at the time when the then president of Mexico, General Lázaro Cárdenas, expropriated the oil interests that British, some Dutch, and American companies had there. And that meant that it was a very daring thing to do. And I think what Ricardo [López Méndez], my uncle, tried to do with his poem was to try to galvanize some "intellectual" support and not just political support of that move. Ricardo went on to write other poems that were also of an epic sort, in terms of history. He has what I consider his best poem, a very beautiful poem, to the city of Mérida, in Yucatán, and its history. In any case, I don't know whether he might be considered a first influence in a bodily way, because my mother, who was a very sensitive person, very much given to cultural things and aesthetics—she had started out to be a pianist, and then after she married my father, she gave that up (as a career, that is). She didn't give up playing at home, but she gave it up as a possible career. She also took up ballet in her spare time. She was much given to reading, and I picked up from her the love of books and reading—not just poetry, but prose, fiction, and so forth.

My father was a military man, and he was totally the opposite—not in the sense that they didn't gibe, but in that he was just a different personality with a different tendency and different interests. And from him, in terms of any kind of cultural things, I picked up more the issue of history. History was his thing.

So this was Mexico City, and because my father was gradually drawing away from active service in the army, in the Mexican armed forces, he began to develop what he wanted to do in the northern part of Mexico, and that is agriculture, cattle raising, everything that he could put together not only to make a business of it but also to benefit the country where he had been born.

My mother was born in central Mexico. Her father was a German immigrant first to the United States and then to Mexico, with the American Smelting Company. He found a woman he liked down there, married and had eight children: five girls, three boys. Two of them died very young. The other one died much later. But the women, the daughters of that family, were actually more significant than the men.

And since my father began this ranch operation on the border—I was eleven years old, I guess—I was sent to school in the States, in Texas, in San Antonio. After high school, I told my father that I did not expect to pick up a military career: not that he expected me to, but I wanted to let him know ahead of time. He did, however, want me to be an engineer. He was an army engineer, and he wanted me to be an engineer, so I did in fact register in the school of engineering at the University of Texas. After two years, I realized that was not for me, and I told him so. I said, "I can do it, but I won't be a good engineer, and I won't particularly like it." So he said, "Well, then do whatever you want to."

And by that time, I had met, through a roommate of mine from Monterrey, Mexico, a Spanish professor in what was then the Romance Languages Department: Professor Ramón Martínez López. And I began to take courses that he offered. He had a friend in the English department, Professor Robert Clarence Stephenson, who was doing what later would become—except with all the hoopla of theory—comparative literature. He gave courses in translation from French, Russian, and Spanish. Of course, since he could pick up graduate students in Spanish; he knew Spanish well enough to give those courses in Spanish. But it was harder to find people who knew Russian, so he gave those in translation. And French: I remember taking his course on Proust, which was wonderful.

Well, all this has brought me to the point of what I felt like doing of my own, because of where I was and what I was studying, either literature in Spanish *or* sometimes even *more* urgently, in English. I took graduate courses in English, nineteenth-century authors such as Byron, Shelley, Keats, Wordsworth, Coleridge, Lee Hunt, all those, from very good professors. And that's why one of my very first poems ["To Spring"] . . . if there's any influence patent in a poem, there it is. The British Romantics.

DAC: But that was written before you started college? Am I right?

MGG: No, I was here. Nineteen years old.

DAC: In the winter of 1950 you won the Award for Creative Writing at the University of Texas. Was it for that poem?

MGG: For a group.

DAC: A portfolio of poems?

MGG: Yes.

DAC: So why the Romantics? You said your studies in literature were varied, some in Spanish, some in English, other works in translation from different languages, French; but what was it about the British Romantic poets that took such a hold on you? Was it Professor Stephenson, or maybe someone else, who emphasized their aesthetic value in a way that impressed you?

MGG: Right. That was Professor Willis Pratt, who was a specialist in the Romantics. Now, it was about this time that I decided to take odd jobs to support myself, and not depend any more on my father.

I wanted to go to Greenwich Village.

But I couldn't afford it because I thought, "Will I get there, and will it be as easy to get odd jobs over there as it is in Austin?" Well, it wouldn't have been; I would have been out of place. So I didn't make it over there, I just visited. At the same time, I must admit, for so many years, until I was eleven years old, I was speaking only Spanish. So Spanish was a stronger linguistic base for me, I must admit. And then came Professor Martínez López, with his Generation of '98 and Generation of '27 and so on.

Also, as a Mexican, and through my mother, I was reading Spanish-American poets—not just the Spanish peninsular poets, but the Spanish-American poets, and Mexican poets. For instance, one of the Mexican poets that Tita [Valencia] and I constantly remember and refer to and read is Ramón López Velarde, who influenced Pablo Neruda. And there is, I think, for my Spanish poetry, a significant influence from López Velarde, not so much in themes, but in prosody.

DAC: Do you think that the Spanish poets of the Generation of '27 and the British Romantic poets of the nineteenth century match well? Do you think that they have a comparable sensibility? It seems like there has been a tendency in some writers who read across the languages to find something kindred in them. Is there? Is it maybe the posing of philosophical questions, the thinking in abstractions?

MGG: That's an awfully good question that I'm not sure I can answer, *but* I can do this: I can give an example of what might be [a cross-section, or sampling] . . . In Spanish, the word is *cala*, which is something that, in maritime exploration, you insert to go down in the water to test what's below. What I'm referring to is this: One of the, I think, really wonderful poets, not *nearly* as well known a poet as García Lorca, because García Lorca was a miracle, but I'm talking about Luis Cernuda. He had, for some reason, a sensibility toward English, so he wrote a study of English Romantic poets. Now, here comes another bit of irony: comes the Spanish Civil War, he has to go, like so many. Unfortunately, Lorca didn't [leave], and that's why he was killed. And Cernuda goes to England and he tries to establish a rapport—guess with whom? T. S. Eliot. It doesn't work.

DAC: Why not?

MGG: Well, Eliot didn't know Spanish. And he relied on other exiled Spaniards regarding the then contemporary values in literature. And the people he consulted, either for reasons of envy, or for other reasons of lack of friendship, did not give their stamp of approval to the questions that Eliot had, in order to publish translations of these people. So not many got translated or published.

So Cernuda, he was a problem. And this is strange. It seems this is not by any means so prevalent now. But in the thirties, it was still operating, and it was not only in Spain or Latin America, but even in England and the United States. And that is the censure of homosexuality. And Cernuda was an avowed homosexual. He was not the only one. So was Lorca. So was Aleixandre. But they were in the closet. So that's another possibility. I don't know how strong a motive that was, but then maybe also just a matter of a different sensibility.

But you asked about why Spanish poets of the '27 may be interested in English *Romantics*. And they were interested in T. S. Eliot, no question about it. And Joyce.

DAC: I asked that question very honestly because I'm not really sure, even though in some of the prose, and some manifestos of the early twentieth-century avant-gardes of Latin America and Spain, there was clearly a lot of language borrowed from Imagism and Vorticism and Futurism and Surrealism by a lot of modernist groups in Argentina and Spain.

MGG: Right.

DAC: And Lorca himself wrote many of the manifestos and defenses of *ultraísmo* and other factions of *la vanguardia* that seemed to be borrowing from the language of Imagism and "direct treatment of the thing," cutting out "superfluous language": using imagery, imagery of the world around us, the modern world, the city, machines, and technology. And yet there seems to be such a preoccupation with philosophy and the metaphysical that I think maybe that's a way into how it connects with the Romantics. But I guess what this brings me to is a question about *your* work, which is the role of philosophical thought in some of your poetry. It doesn't seem that it's just Romanticism and the Generation of '27 manifesting itself in your poetry. There are obviously reaches to contemporary and avant-garde images, Anglo modernists and others—even, I would say, confessional poets. But I want to get to the question of philosophy in some of your work.

MGG: You yourself are interested in philosophy, is that it?

DAC: No, I want to see if *you* are interested in philosophy. Do you think that poetry starts with a question? Can poetry answer philosophical questions? Or do poetry and philosophy rub up against each other in ways that can eliminate the other? There are several of your poems, some of the short ones, some of the longer ones, that seem to pose themselves in philosophical language—sometimes very explicitly invoking Heidegger or Sartre, philosophers you've obviously read—but also cast themselves as a means to answering these questions. So: Can poetry answer questions that are meaningful to philosophy?

MGG: Well, let me say this. I tend more to be in agreement with another poet, much closer to our times and who died not too long ago, who was, to a certain extent, a mentor of mine—what we would call in Spanish *maestro*. And that's Octavio Paz. And I tend to agree with him when he says, "Poetry does not give answers; it poses questions." More than answers, it poses questions: not explicitly, necessarily, but implicitly. What is the nature of poetry?

You know, it has been thought that painters, in order to do what they do, must use a canvas. And musicians, that is, composers—what do they use instead of canvas? Silence. Poetry combines these things in some ways because fiction writers (and philosophers)—what do they use? The human mind. That's what they write on. Painters use colors and brushes. Composers use notes and instruments. And writers use words. And where do they write the words? Well sure, instead of on canvas or the so-called silence, they have paper or a computer, what have you. But what do they use? Words. And the words themselves gather into forms and produce sounds. So how much does a poet or writer of fiction deal with philosophy? I think they—both the writer of fiction and the poet—are more *influenced* by philosophy than *users* of philosophy. It's something that goes into his activity. Roland Barthes described what he did as an activity. That's what it is [*poesis*]. You might not have to use your hands or a chisel or a hammer or other kinds of tools, but it's an activity.

Of course I'm here eighty-two years old going on eighty-three, but even *much* younger writers today are not only influenced by modernism, and then existentialism, *and* science; still they're influenced by Romanticism. I think when Romanticism grew and produced the creations that it did, no matter in what genre, it was searching very deeply into, for want of a better phrase, what they called the human soul. And that may be why modern poets like the Spanish Generation of '27 or other *modernistas* in Spanish America still went back to Romanticism. López Velarde goes back to Romanticism. But by that time, there is something else to be found and to be reckoned with. It's not the explosion of emotions of Romanticism. Along with those emotions, there is beginning to be more carefulness. And that carefulness, to me—or at least in terms of what you've been asking about influences—has been exemplified by the French symbolists. One of the poets who didn't write all that much (I mean, he wasn't a Victor Hugo) but what he did was so central to the modern, was Mallarmé. Baudelaire, Verlaine, Mallarmé. And those that come later: Apollinaire and the rest of the French. So that's another influence that you would have to find in what I've done. And let's face it, they influenced Eliot himself.

DAC: Sure. Influenced Pound, too.

MGG: No doubt about it.

DAC: The transformation from symbol to image, moving in a way from the prescription of what a symbol would be to an open-ended raw image unprescriptive and unprescribed but certainly emotive… this change in tendency had great impact.

MGG: D. H. Lawrence, as critic, has a great phrase: "Images of myth are symbols." And you can go backwards. You can find the symbol and ask, "Where did *that* come from?" Well, there was a myth somewhere behind it. This is in *Essays in American Literature*, I think.

DAC: In your collection *The Brandywine in Winter and Other Poems,* you have a grouping of poems devoted to Anglo modernists—

MGG: Pound, Eliot, Stevens.

DAC: And Philip Larkin in the poem "Larkining."

MGG: Yes.

DAC: So obviously at some time when you were writing the other poems of *The Brandywine in Winter* you were thinking about modernists, Anglo modernists.

MGG: I guess, to some extent, sure.

DAC: But in looking at your work, did you ever consider modernist aesthetics in terms of pushing the forms that you yourself would inhabit as a poet to become more contiguous with what modernists were doing, moving away from lyricism, moving away and into true free verse, without sustained or repeated patterns in prosody?

MGG: That's true, getting away from strict forms, *but*, what I think came from my reading of the English and even American modernists was more thematic than formal. I think the formal definitely was just free verse. And in that collection you may have noticed there *are* one or two or three poems that go back to strict form. And in *The Musicians*, the poem itself, "The Musicians," is strict form. One of the things that I enjoyed when I did things like that was finding rhymes.

For instance, the poem "Black on White." If anything, that poem is . . . I don't know if I can call it this, but an example of virtuosity. How many other Spanish speakers can use the English language like that? I think it's only natural that the poet tends to use the language he knows best to write his poetry. Then how is it that I sometimes crawl out of the window to use another language? Oh, crawling out a window reminds me—about your questions on philosophy—[the Spanish poet] Antonio Machado, in a prose piece, says that poets, as opposed to philosophers, when they run into a dead end, instead of trying to solve the dead end philosophically, crawl out into the sky. Something like that. Fly.

DAC: You brought up "Black on White" in *The Musicians and Other Poems*. And I was thinking about why modernist or avant-garde sensibilities in English poetry don't really manifest in so many poems. But in "Soliloquy with Echoes"—I wouldn't call it a prose poem; it's lineated and it's not prose—but the lines are long, the tone is a bit more casual.

MGG: Definitely.

DAC: You've abandoned formally the capitals, using capital letters at the beginning of lines, the beginning of sentences. And it feels like talking sometimes, a kind of talking to yourself.

MGG: Yes! There's a narrative quality to it, isn't there?

DAC: Yes. I'll read it.

MGG: Sure.

DAC: "Soliloquy With Echoes."

the vast window of morning opens to a solitary world.
before perception lie the manifold investitures
of ageless echoes, and now to act. but wait, first
to reflect upon the sundry happenings of yesterday
and of the day before, this is the proper way, the careful
way: start the day right, they always say. perhaps
if we could hear those words again: how many days?
it will be here tomorrow. do you love me? sir,
we are sorry to inform you . . . for heaven's sake, let
the cash register ring. or should the church bells ring?
for time is made of money and life is made of time, and
strictly speaking, yes, that's right, life is worth living.

no, let's start again. yes, yes, from scratch.
the window of the morning opens to a lonely world.
before my eyes lie the wakened streets, a modicum of snow,
a small variety of old misshapen cars. get up. it should
be said in exclamation, and now to act. the world
is cruelly waiting though the sun is not yet out. motions,
gestures, all rehearsed before a mirror: to the left, to the right,
up and down, here and there, coming, coming. ready?
for heaven's sake, just why so fast? let's think, let
us reflect. we must have time, we all need time.

so, let's start again. yes, from the top.
my window opens to a world that's all alone. the streets

are practically the same as always. there's not much
difference between today and yesterday or even day before.
get up! what for? it's new year's day in paradise.
the world, the world turns without us. we do have time
to think and to reflect. the ring of money and the ring
of time are alien to us now. perhaps, then, we can hear
those words again: do you love me? yes, i love you. yes,
forever. tomorrow is today. sir, we are sorry to inform
you . . . no! let's start again. what's that you say? there
is no time? the window of the morning opens to the night.

This seems to stand out to me, among so many of your other poems, as a poem that is almost trying to communicate something: is taking a tone or form that is inviting in a kind of casual, vulnerable, human, private but not guarded kind of way. And it feels to me like a poem that is, in diction and style, more contemporary; it doesn't have that weight of preserving a notion of a higher quality of tradition that so many of your poems have. I wouldn't say it has a "man on the street" kind of quality, but it certainly seems less performed, in a way, less rendered to a standard of verse tradition that I think so many of your poems do have—the formal ones. I actually balk at calling some of them not formal, because I think all of your poems are formal—some don't rhyme and some do; sometimes the metrics are sustained, sometimes not. But there's form to all of them, and they're all formalist in a way. But "Soliloquy With Echoes" stands out.

My question is: What's unique about this poem? What was unique about writing that poem, and why do you not have more poems like that?

MGG: Mainly because I consciously wanted to do the formal instead. But you discovered something very interesting and very true here, that it suggests an invitation—an invitation to what? Because its language is colloquial, it's an invitation to peer into inner desolation, as I see it now, after you read it.

DAC: In "Soliloquy with Echoes," you've managed to embed an "I" in the poem with limited use of the "I." And the echoes, it's interesting, the starting again, to start and restart. In a way, I think a lot of poets (maybe you feel the same way) always feel that impetus to start a new poem, again and again. And oftentimes you're satisfied or dissatisfied with the product, and maybe that's part of the drive to keep writing—when you write a poem and you're not totally satisfied with it, or it leaves something out, it makes you want to start again. But the starting over, the starting and then the digression, and then the hint of despair, and then the confusion that it renders. And then: "All right, let me start again." Erase that, start over again. You know, it's like a chalkboard: you erase it, but all the chalk dust is still muddying the board. And that's kind of what it feels like in the starting again. But there is this vulnerability: you called it inner desolation, but there seems to be this vulnerability that is . . . it seems to be somewhat rare, because other times in your poems it feels like there is a drive to preserve, to capture or—well, not so much to capture, but to put into words a frame of mind, an idea, and in a sense to preserve it, to press the petals into the page.

MGG: Exactly. Exactly.

DAC: And in preserving it, someone can go back and revisit that state of mind, that idea, that feeling in the language. So I guess one question is: Wordsworth said the poet is "a man speaking to men," and talked about poetry in terms of it really as a form of expression, that in a way has a communicative value to it—

MGG: But remember "Emotions Recollected in Tranquility"? One of the criticisms, friendly criticisms, that was leveled against me by a man that I liked very much, admired very much, a poet, now deceased, James Colin Murphy, said, "But Miguel, you don't use language which is reader-friendly." Now, I think the poem you just read had language that is reader-friendly. And my answer to him was, "But I think that the poet should be the guardian of language, and therefore continue to use language insofar as it is feasible, convenient, effective, and that may come from centuries past." My ideal has always been the crystal.

And a poem should somehow crystallize a thought or feeling through images. An image itself should be crystalline.

DAC: The poet-critic, Annie Finch, in 1999, published a collection of essays called *After New Formalism*, and in her preface, she uses the term "multi-formalism." And by that she means the "new formalist" poets, a term which had been referencing mostly poets writing in the late seventies into the eighties, when poetry journals started to become a little bit more open to publishing sonnets, rhymed verse, forms of lyric. She used the term multi-formalism as opposed to new formalism, because the contemporary poet who writes formal verse has all the history of forms available. When you said that the poet is a "guardian of language" and that the language may come from centuries past, do you feel that when you write, are you picking and choosing elements of tone? Do you *construct* a tone to your poems? Or do you feel like you have a certain default tone that you revert to when you get into the mood of writing a poem? Do you think that there is a default tone that you have, that you tap when you write? Or do you feel, depending on the subject matter, like you will choose a tone or construct a tone that is appropriate to what you're trying to express?

MGG: I think [default tone] happens to me more in Spanish than in English because after all, English is less of a natural language for me than Spanish, more of a learned language than Spanish. With Spanish, this is what almost invariably happens to me, and this is going to sound strange: I let language lead me, rather than a priori construction of a linguistic approach to the poem. Whenever I get the sense that I have something to say in verse, I begin and then I feel if that language is the one. With English, because, as I say, I began to learn it when I was eleven years old, I tend to be more careful.

* * *

DAC: Can you explain your perspective on self-translation? How, in your own life and experience, do language barriers and different domains of language tie in to national barriers and your own personal experience as both a Mexican and an American? I think it's interesting that in your poetry you don't really get bilingual. You don't code switch, ever.

MGG: *Ever*. Well, the reason I don't mix the languages, I don't code switch, is that my conviction is that poetry resides in the language. And to try to, or to want to make it reside in two languages at the same time—now this language in one phrase, now this other one in another phrase, or whatever—destroys the genuineness of the poetry. Now, Mexican American poets do all kinds of things, and it's their business. But when I read one of those poems, I don't have the feeling of genuineness—in spite of the fact that it may be there. Poetry resides in the language, and languages have different structures, different sounds. And I'm not going into meaning. There was a professor at SMU by the name of Perine. Did you ever come across his book? *Sound and Sense*.

DAC: Sure.

MGG: Okay. Well, poetry has sound and sense indeed, but it also has form. It *has* to. It just by nature does. I don't care what form it is, whether it's strict form or free verse, it's a form that's part of the whole thing of the poem.

Even just in speaking, I very seldom code switch. If I do, number one, it's intentional. Number two, it's for humor. Or, for instance, in Henry James, you have a lot of French thrown in there all of a sudden, and it's for ornamentation and show. I remember one time an editor in New York, writing a letter to me about something we had going, said, "Please keep me *au courant*." And I said to myself, "Well, that sounds nice, but it's a little much!"

DAC: Is there anything in your education or experience that has shaped this perspective? Because for other poets and other writers, many Chicano poets, say, their linguistic world *is* that. It is mixed in a way that is simultaneous.

MGG: Exactly.

DAC: So why is it that in your world it's preserved?

MGG: Because I preserved it! Simply that. I don't consider myself a Mexican American. And to me, Chicano is really a political thing. But I don't consider myself a Mexican American. I consider myself a Mexican living in the United States. I've thought about it and I may go back to live the rest of my life in Mexico. Who knows? And what I've brought here, I brought from Mexico. And what I take back with me I will take from the United States. But I'm a Mexican *Mexican*. In fact, I'm a Mexican citizen. I never have become an American citizen. Call it patriotism, call it laziness, I don't know what.

I think that Mexican Americans speak their language because that's what they have been thrust into, to express themselves—whether they're writers or non-writers. I don't know whether the writers (and there again, it depends on the individual, I'm sure) do this consciously or unconsciously. I know that the non-writer does it unconsciously. They don't make it a point to say, "*tengo* two shoes," like that—but they do! And whether the writer does that in honor of his experience, *experiencia*, or does it like the non-writer, just unconsciously, I don't know. But I know if I'm thinking in Spanish, I go on in Spanish. If I'm thinking in English, I go on in English. And I don't see the point of mixing. I don't *have* to. And as I said, I think it's the main reason poetry resides in the language. And you can't reside in two places at the same time. You can move from one to the other, but not at the same time.

DAC: On the point of nationality and nationhood, did you feel that when you began to write English poetry, it was a tradition that you felt ownership of, in the sense that you were writing *in* the tradition, or did you feel like you were writing yourself *into* the tradition?

MGG: I have been told [of some of my poetry], "But that's not English poetry, that's not traditional," to which I replied, "No, I guess it isn't." And thinking about it, I come to the conclusion that perhaps I'm only on the edge of tradition in English, and perhaps only on the edge, though perhaps closer to the edge, of tradition in Spanish. Perhaps I don't really have a tradition that is fixed and recognizable.

I think somebody who is strictly a Spanish poet or critic will say that I don't fit the patterns of Spanish traditional poetry—just as this man told me. Of course he was only speaking about those very brief loose poems of *The Infinite Absence.* But I think unless you make or try to make a case *for* the strict rhymed and metered—whether it be "The Musicians," or "Familiar Stranger"—[you run into something else] . . . an example of something I was talking about earlier, and that is the poem that is written starting from an element of spontaneity, as opposed to the poem that is labored, if not belabored, into a pattern that is strict in meter and rhyme and so forth. It's two different things: the spontaneous, of course, is most likely to be free verse.

DAC: So which kind is the title poem of *The Brandywine in Winter and Other Poems?*

MGG: That poem was done in two stages. There is the reprint from *Texas Quarterly* which had half of it, and then afterwards I wrote the second part, made it two parts. How that came about was that living in Pennsylvania at the time, my wife [Betty] and I went on a visit to Chadds Ford, Pennsylvania, where Andrew Wyeth lived. And apart from visiting his place, we went driving in different areas of the nearby countryside. And I got out of the car and went down, camera in hand, and looked at two or three views of the stream/brook Brandywine, and took photographs there. I still have one in our bungalow. I had some blown up, and I had it in front of me, where I had a desk, and one day I was sitting there—I don't know what I was doing, reading, thinking—and I looked up and I saw that, and I told myself, "Dadgum, I'm gonna write something about this!" So the photograph preceded that. And I wrote that first part. And then years later, when I was going to put together this collection of poems—which was done, incidentally, by a small group of people, a designer, a printer, and myself, and I was footing most of the bill for paper and so on—I thought to myself, "I want to expand that," so I wrote the second half.

So what can *you* tell me about it?

DAC: I like the cadence, I like how it unfolds. I like how it works at the beginning: "Water and ice, the stream unfolds, / / Still, moving, moving still, not desolate." By the way, that "still, moving, moving still": that mirroring of phrase happens in a *lot* of your poems.

MGG: Right.

DAC: I wouldn't say it's really a device, but it is something that I've noticed in many poems. I thought this would be a poem that would exemplify it. It's a good example of your unrhymed verse, with many of the themes and concerns that you have in other poems—

MGG: Nature.

DAC: Nature, solitude.

MGG: And in this case, history thrown in there.

DAC: There's a poet-critic, Dana Gioia, who has been a defender of contemporary formalist poetry from the eighties until now, who wrote a piece that makes a distinction between early twentieth-century formalists who were writing at the turn of the century while some of their contemporaries were innovating avant-garde tendencies in poetry, what many called "open form," open poetry—

MGG: Open, yes.

DAC: And Gioia makes a distinction between those earlier formalists writing traditional verse in the avant-garde moment and the poets in the seventies and eighties who started to turn back to formalist poetry *after* free verse and open poetry had become the norm.

MGG: Exactly—the norm, the order of the day.

DAC: So what had become institutionalized, if you will, as academic poetry, were the descendants of Williams and Pound and Objectivist poets like Louis Zukovsky and Charles Olsen. Then the students of these poets, and the *students* of the students of these poets—

MGG: Right, generations.

DAC: They just saw open poetry and open forms as what poetry *was*. And then when younger poets started, in the seventies and eighties, to decide to revisit sonnets and villanelles and sestinas, they were being dissuaded and even chastised by mentors, academic professors, poets, who believed that that was all antiquated and retrograde and not what new poetry should be. In fact, some viewed it as particularly un-American.

MGG: Political!

DAC: And polemical. There was this rhetoric of it being classified as a kind of Reaganite poetics, linked to the neo-conservatism of when Ronald Reagan became president. A liberal backlash against neo-formalism that tried to argue the case of self-preservation in political terms. But really, Dana Gioia and others have put forth the case very well that it wasn't so much that as it was this idea, as Annie Finch said, of multi-formalism. We have all these forms of poetry that are available to us, from the medieval to the present, and they're available, they're all versions of the English language, and it's all in the palette of the English language. Poets have the right—

MGG: Democracy!

DAC: Yes, to choose. And also, one distinction that Gioia makes is that the new formalist, the neo-formalist poets use antiquated or inherited forms, but express contemporary themes.

MGG: Right.

DAC: Things that couldn't *possibly* have been discussed in the nineteenth century—or the sixteenth century, for that matter—because there was no possibility of that reality.

MGG: Right.

DAC: And I think your poem, "Familiar Stranger," in the setting of the wild West Texas wind, defamiliarizes the setting enough for it to feel like, "Okay, well obviously this isn't America, this isn't the Southwest." And historically speaking, that in and of itself is very new.
MGG: That's topographical, as a matter of fact.

DAC: It *is* topographical. Also [figuratively] in the rhymed quatrains. The details on a micro level are very tightly rendered: "Gray feathers from the nests under the eaves / Were blown away by wild West Texas wind."

MGG: That's alliteration.

DAC: It's alliteration, and it's consonance also: "away" and "blown" where the consonance is buried. "Were blown away by wild West Texas wind." So I thought that was a very carefully written poem, and it reminds me of "This Round of Twelve."

MGG: In "This Round of Twelve," I wanted to end with a beginning. Because the reference is round, it's the clock and other wheels and things. You should do a poem the same. You should not end and stop, but go back to the beginning again.

DAC: Okay. Do you like it?

MGG: Not as much as others.

DAC: Okay.

MGG: It was…what shall we say?…"a pretty thing."

DAC: Do you think that all of your poems are finished?

MGG: No. Some are, and some are not.

DAC: The ones that you've published?

MGG: Of the ones that I've published, some are finished, and some are not. Like I think I said before, maybe they just remain as projects of poems.

DAC: Would you ever go back to them?

MGG: Probably not. I'd rather do something else, maybe. I don't know. It would be hard to tell. A friend of mine published, in Spain, my collection *Palabras inútiles*. In the binding, I said maybe these are just unfinished projects. That I might like to return to and revise, but others, which I feel are farther behind in my experience, I would just as soon just let go as maybe not really successful or as successful as I'd like them to be.

I want to read just a paragraph here [from *Burnt Orange Britannia*], which had to do with something you said. "After high school I went back to Mexico for two years. I worked for an uncle who had an advertising agency." (Incidentally, this is the uncle who was a poet, Ricardo López Méndez.) "I read voluminously, and I reacquainted myself with my country, Mexico. But apart from having a good time, I was actually floundering. Even my uncle told me so. A poet himself, he suspected my literary leanings. I considered studying law at the National Autonomous University of Mexico, but the recollection of my experience in the United States had become a lure. The librarian at the Texas Military Institute, a dear lady named Miss George, who also had perceived how much I liked literature, had suggested I apply for entrance to Washington and Lee. It was in the miniscule library at the Texas Military Institute that I started writing poetry in English, encouraged by Miss George and Professor Barrett, the latter praising me mildly for my feeble attempts to follow in the steps of Poe and Robert Louis Stevenson, in both verse and prose fiction. But my secret pastime was to imitate those English poets who wrote short yet demanding forms, like the French medieval rondeaux and rondels, with their variant refrains. Little did I know that years later I would find reflections of them in Joyce's *Chamber Music*."

You see, in English, I tend to be more careful [than in Spanish]. Sometimes, because of that, I manage to be more inventive. Perhaps that inventiveness turns out to be artificial: How much is poetry natural, and how much is it artificial? And when I say artificial, I don't mean it pejoratively. I think there's a lot of artifice to art. So in terms of creativity in poetry, there has to be a difference between what I do when I write in Spanish and what I do when I write in English. Sometimes I feel that I have achieved something, and sometimes I feel that I simply "did it," and it's there. Last night I was thinking that poems are like children. And there's something in my own critical terms that makes me *feel* that some are simply better than others.

DAC: So when composing in English or in Spanish, do you feel like you're *performing* in English, or performing a version of English, as opposed to in Spanish, where it feels more expressive? Does one tap more your formal education, while the other taps something more primal, if you will?

MGG: Let me approach the question and subject from a different angle—circumstances. I would like to think that having learned English to the extent that I can write poetry, it should be the same whether I write a poem in English or I write a poem in Spanish. Can we base that on theory or just wishful thinking? I think the circumstances have a lot to do with it. I'll elaborate.

When I wrote *Palabras inútiles*, my first wife [Betty Brumbalow] had died of a brain tumor in 1982. I felt that I wanted to write poems about her, to her, as if speaking to her. She was an English speaker. She was a Texas girl. So why did I write in Spanish? When I started writing, it came out in Spanish [. . .] It was something going down deep inside of me and coming back out from those depths of emotion. That's why I said circumstances. Here it was, suddenly roiled up emotions come out in Spanish. Does that prove what you've been saying, that English for me, as an instrument of poetic expression, is more formal: not so natural? Of course there's a possible contradiction. The poem "Soliloquy With Echoes," which you already have noticed, appears only in English.

DAC: "The Space of Night" was—

MGG: Dedicated to Hazel Ransom.

DAC: Was it written after she died?

MGG: Yes.

DAC: Why the "space" of night?

MGG: In other words, the black; the darkness of night is really the darkness of death.

* * *

DAC: I'd like to continue by asking you about specific poems that stood out to me for one reason or another.

MGG: Sure.

DAC: Tell me about "Dance of the White Lady."

MGG: You seem to like that one.

DAC: I really do.

MGG: I do too.

DAC: I think it's a very good poem. Is this form one that you found?

MGG: No, I just made it up.

DAC: Is that what motivated you to write it? That you wanted to write a poem that invents its own sustained form?

MGG: I can tell you the background of several poems, but not all. Let's see if I can pick this out of my memory. What does the epigraph say?

DAC: It says, "In Teutonic mythology, the White Ladies were a kind of fairies. When the castle of Neuhaus was built, one appeared in 1628 dressed in white with a bunch of keys at her side, and said she was waiting for judgment; on another occasion she announced that it was ten o'clock. In Normandy the White Ladies lurk in ravines, fords, bridges and other narrow passes and on Maundy Thursday ask passengers to dance. The most famous is La Dame D'Aprigny, who used to inhabit the site of the present Rue St. Quentin, at Bayeux. (Abridged from Benet's *The Reader's Encyclopedia*, second edition.)"

MGG: That must have been it—simply what I perceived visually as a composite of [this reference], and I liked the idea of a woman in white.

DAC: How did it wind up taking this form, though?

MGG: Please remind me how it starts.

DAC: It starts, "Such dreadful spite between day and night." This is the first line of the first stanza, the second line of the second stanza, the third line of the third stanza, the fourth line of the fourth stanza, the fifth line of the fifth stanza. And then you have a sixth stanza. The first and the sixth are six lines each. The middle four are five lines each. And in the last stanza, *its* last line is the same last line as the first stanza: "The hands of the clock turn the key to the lock."

MGG: Yes. A key turns, the clock turns. The repetition of "Such dreadful spite between day and night" is for emphasis: that there is always a conflict between day and night, light and dark, and I wanted to set this idea against the mythology of the White Lady.

DAC: Okay. Tell me about "Wild Surmise."

MGG: That's for Harry Ransom and his Humanities Research Center.

DAC: The imagery is allusive, ending with the line, "As once on Darien peak now Texas plain."

MGG: Darien peak of course comes from [John Keats's] "On First Looking into Chapman's Homer," in which he refers to "stout Cortez, when with eagle eyes / He stared at the Pacific—and all his men / Look'd at each other with a wild surmise— / Silent, upon a peak in Darien." Of course, mistaking Balboa for Cortez, but Darien peak is in Panamá. In other words, he was seeing another world, and here in this Texas plain the [Harry Ransom Humanities Research Center] is showing us another world.

DAC: What about the poem "New England"?

MGG: Dedicated "To Anne."

DAC: You open the poem with the lines, "The quality of feeling / Was developed in a scene from Robert Frost." Is the scene from "The Road Not Taken"?

MGG: This was in upstate New York, but yes. This poem goes with the new poems, "Three Poems for Nena," written in 2001. Nena is an anagram for Anne. You'll find colloquial approach to the writing of poetry in those poems more so than the others.

DAC: Who is Anna Marzorati?

MGG: A former colleague here [at the University of Texas] but she's in Italy now. She was teaching Italian conversation with a partner in French and Italian. We met and we liked each other, but that's all it was. It has remained a loving friendship, which is wonderful. There're no regrets and no recriminations and this, that, and the other [. . .]

And so Anna is the Italian, and Anne is a girl from [the Midwest].

DAC: Besides "Three Poems for Nena," do you have any other unpublished poems that you might have sent as gifts or letters to anyone?

MGG: No. I have some unpublished poems, but not of that type. They're [mostly] just thoughts that came to my mind, images. One that's kind of relevant to a place which I love and have been to several times, and we had planned to go again this year, *but* we can't, because of commitments in Mexico and so on. And I'm talking about Venice. There's a poem that's a kind of a description of that. Let's see, what else? Well, another poem which you have, which is *not* in the books but was published in a magazine, one that, *I* think, comes as close to working well in both English and Spanish, as any. And that's called "The Edge of Things." It was originally written in Spanish, but I think the English came out *almost* as an original. It was published in *The Dirty Goat*.

DAC: I did read that issue of *The Dirty Goat*, at your suggestion, along with the pieces in *Literary Austin*—your piece and the two pieces on Borges. Hazel Ransom's piece captivated me, so I'm tempted to ask more about her. Your friendship with her seemed very deep.

MGG: She was a friend *way* back when. By the time that I met her, she had married Harry Ransom. She was his student here at UT. And by the time I met her—because I met her through *him*—I'd taken a course with him and we were friends. Then when Dr. Ransom died, she needed—well, she sought my help to edit some things of his that had not been published in book form before. They had been published in magazines, but they had not been published in book form. And so she published, let's see, one, two, three—three books, three collections, of a sort of academic paper. They were not literary. They were from the point of view of a university administrator. One is called *The Conscience of the University*, the other one is called *The Other Texas Frontier*, and the third one is called *Chronicles of Opinion*. Then she published/edited a short collection of texts having to do with this university as a place, and thinking of it in the usual terms. The book is called *Snow in Austin*. And finally, she published a collection of poems that Dr. Ransom wrote in the course of his life. So she asked me to help with those things. And I did. So here she was a widow. And then my wife died—I think I told you, of a brain tumor.

DAC: Yes.

MGG: And a year after that, Hazel invited me to things and to her house. And she was very affectionate. She had reason to be lonely. She and I were both widowed, and we were good friends, so we grew close and ultimately we were together for ten years. And then she got ill. First cardiovascular, then cancer, and so she died. That was another big loss. By that time I had already met Tita, and a year later—Hazel died in '93—in '94 I said to Tita, "Let's get married." We did! We had a beautiful wedding in Mexico, in a place called Amatlán de Quetzalcóatl, in a little country chapel. And I've been happy with her for fifteen years. But anyway, you were asking about Hazel.

DAC: Yes. One thing that struck me about her piece is that she was candid and unassuming, but her tone is so proper.

MGG: Yes. Well, she was extremely proper. I guess she had learned to be that way, being a faculty/high administrator's wife, you know.

DAC: Yes, I imagine. It also reminded me, thinking of your work, about your poetry, and your voice—if I can use the word. Is it all right if I describe your work and say that I think that there's a voice to it?

MGG: Oh, of course! I think a poet has very much of a voice.

DAC: I think so. Poets and critics alike have different views on that.

MGG: Well, I'm sure!

DAC: But I think that there's definitely a voice to all of your poems, even when they vary in form and subject matter and so on, as if there is a voice that does hold them together.

MGG: There was a professor of English here. I never had any courses with him, but I knew him. His name was Ernest Lovell, and he was a Byron specialist, and wrote a book on Byron's correspondence, and called it *His Very Self and Voice*. So he had that idea too.

* * *

DAC: The poem in *The Musicians and Other Poems*, "Involution." Was there an experience that you had, or was it just something you were envisioning?

MGG: I've always thought, without any basis, just a feeling, maybe sentimental—and not that I've studied anything about it, you know, when there's probably a whole school of psychologists who have broached animal psychology—that the human being, having the trouble that it has with the psychologist, and having the brain analyze itself, by the same token doesn't know *everything* that there is to know about the brains and emotions of animals. And of course I guess it's been thought and repeated and maybe accepted that the apes are closer to us than other mammals. So having visited a number of zoological gardens, I've watched gorillas. And I think that there's something impenetrable, and that's why this poem. That's the only reason. Evolution, involution.

DAC: And the lines... Well, if I could just read it—

MGG: Sure.

DAC: Because I think the prosody is really very good, too.
"Involution."
I feel you think. What are you think-
ing, eyes thus crucibled in black?

Is it that you have known the link
Of which some claim there is no track?
In Heraclitus's stream we sink,
You in a cage, I on a rack.
You look at me. I look at you,
Gorilla gorilla gorilla.
We show embarrassment, we who
Are between Charybdis and Scylla.

The line "Gorilla gorilla gorilla," without commas…?

MGG: It's what I saw in the label on the cage. Apparently that is the zoological description, the zoological definition.

DAC: As family, genus, and species, right?

MGG: Yes, there you are.

DAC: Ah. Okay.

MGG: The repetition made it strange, didn't it?

DAC: It did. So this poem came [from a personal experience]. Is the same true for the poem, "Solstitial Birthday Celebration"?

MGG: Oh yes. That's about my mother.

DAC: And your mother was a musician. You have a lot of poems about music.

MGG: Well, I love music.

DAC: Do you think a lot of that stems from your mother?

MGG: I think so. And now Tita.

DAC: Right, who's also a pianist.

MGG: Yes.

DAC: But your mother played music at home quite a bit?

MGG: Oh yes.

DAC: Were they special occasions or spur-of-the-moment?

MGG: No, no, just practicing and so on.

DAC: Your parents would entertain and she would play?

MGG: She would play—very seldom that I recall—not many times. It was all practice.

* * *

DAC: I like very much the poem "Moonscape," even though it's so small.

MGG: Read it to me, because I don't remember it.

DAC: "Moonscape."

In the hollow where sleeping trees
Surround the dark and quiet pool
And southward blow the autumn lees,
Piercing silence the nightbirds rule,
Drawing the distance with sound. And
Over the watchful hill, high strewn
With stars, the skies submerge the land
In the wake of the sleepflying moon.

MGG: Okay, yes, I remember.

DAC: Was that also just an image from your mind? "Sleepflying"?

MGG: "Sleepflying." From time to time I try to come up with [a portmanteau]. Is it from the same collection that has the Franz Marc poem?

DAC: Yes, "Two Paintings by Franz Marc."

MGG: Yes. The second part, "Deer in the Forest," ends with the line, "The wood is still, and arrowlight the sun."

DAC: [Like "Two Paintings by Franz Marc,"] "Rejoinders" is another poem that [is comprised of two parts and] really has me *very* interested in how you sometimes write in different voices.

MGG: Different voices, yes.

DAC: It's a conversation between Melville, a Second Speaker, a Third Speaker, and Jean-Paul. It's very different from everything else.

MGG: It is! From time to time, I want a change. I don't want to be monotonous, even to myself!

DAC: Do you remember who you had in mind for the different speakers? Because Melville and Jean-Paul are named.

MGG: Yes. And the Other Speaker is always me, I guess.

DAC: Because there's a second, and then there's a third. "Let this cup pass" is spoken by the Third Speaker.

MGG: Well of course that's Christ.

DAC: "But as thou wilt." The Third Speaker in part two is also Christ?

MGG: Yes.

DAC: So it's an author you're reading, and then your response.

MGG: Yes.

DAC: And then Christ.

MGG: Yes. The writer is Thinker, I guess.

DAC: Right. And so it's Herman Melville and Jean-Paul Sartre?

MGG: Yes—*No*, not Sartre. Jean-Paul Richter.

DAC: Oh, Richter. Speaking of clarifying names: Who is Miss K. W. from "In Memoriam, Miss K. W."?

MGG: Katherine Wheatley was her name. She was a professor of French and French literature here at the University of Texas when I was an undergraduate.

DAC: It ends so beautifully.

MGG: I like that.

DAC: The last stanza reads, "And now I come to say the many things / I should have said. For nothing lingers. / Those yellow roses, those roses wither / And fall to pieces through my fingers." That is very—

MGG: Touching.

DAC: Touching. Sincere. And "The Country Nurse"—

MGG: And "The Country Nurse" also.

DAC: It, too, is a very beautiful poem, I think. I like how this one ends as well. Again you take form and give it life by filling the space with something that you've felt and seen, and something that's more contiguous to the reality of an experienced present.

MGG: And some things imagined. You know, a reality that was not physical, but was there.

DAC: So this idea of "The Country Nurse"—were you empathizing with the woman you describe?

MGG: Empathizing with the country life, yes. You asked me before about being someone who writes in Spanish and English, and I'd like to come back to that thought. I don't know how to phrase it in such a way that the Mexican Americans will not take offense. You know, "He does only Spanish, or he does only English, and he doesn't want to be with us." I have my defense, but I don't know that it's something that people are willing or able to understand: that poetry resides in the language, and you just don't go from one house to another in the same poem.

DAC: I think that it would be something that many can handle.

MGG: Did you ever look up the poetry of Rosemary Catacalos?

DAC: I've come across it but I haven't worked on it.

MGG: Well, I'll make the point a different way. In *Brandywine in Winter*, there's the poem, "Ashes of the Dead." Can you read it?

DAC: Sure. "Ashes of the Dead."

When having cried the deeper cry of loneliness
One reappears, such revenant is likely to assume
The aura of a seer. For what he sees
Is not what people speak about, his
Is a narrative which words betray.

What is the purpose of the things we say?

Are the pigeons in the Piazza di San Marco
The same as those around Trafalgar Square?
Somewhere the answer lies and with its truth
Transcends all space so openly confined.
The measure of our love tries to restore
A flesh torn off with iron long ago.
The pious theft must be achieved from time,
Call it a saintly relic, call it what you will,
And celebrate the wonder with the rites of spring,
Refurbished yet, by right of conquest, owned:
The spirit's lust ("We wed thee, oh our sea,
In proof of true and permanent dominion").
The skillful battle must again be fought
Against an enemy in flight but always dangerous
And victory commemorated with a virile stone
("Your country counts on every man doing
His part, thank God I have done mine").

What is the purpose of the things we say?

We say them as a lure, a cat's cradle of sound
To catch the sunlight that will not be caught.
There is no way to really wed the waves or
Win the war, to speak is not reality but art.
Somewhere the whole array of statements falls apart,
A columbarium rendered suddenly agape
Where words, like doves that having nested much too long,
Now break the holy urns and, fluttering, escape.

MGG: Can something that is contrived be made to sound natural? In some ways, this is the most contrived poem I've ever written, starting out with how it began. I was reading a book review somewhere, and this was in the late seventies, before 1980, I think. And in that book review, I came across the word "columbary." So I went to the dictionary, and it told me what it was, and right next to it was the word "columbaria." So a columbarium is this place where the Romans kept funeral urns with ashes of the dead. And "columbary" is a dovecote where doves nest. So I said, "Ashes, doves, and words." Then I began to develop the poem with quotes from [Lord Byron's] *Doge of Venice* and from Lord Horatio Nelson at Trafalgar.

DAC: "Your country counts on every man doing / His part, thank God I have done mine." These are the words of Lord Nelson?

MGG: Yes. And the other quotation is from what the doges had to say, you know. "We wed thee, oh our sea..." See, in other words, Venice is the bride, and the sea is the groom.

* * *

MGG: Moving from one place to another can result in losses. I've lost boxes of books, and that's really what hurts me most. I lost a short novel I had written, in manuscript. This was before there was any photocopying or this kind of thing, you know. It was paper, lost in a box.

DAC: A whole manuscript?

MGG: A whole manuscript, a short novel.

DAC: Do you think it's possible it might be buried in files or storage?

MGG: No, no, no, it's just been too long ago.

DAC: Wow. What was it about?

MGG: It was called *Conversation Between Twilights*. And it had to do with a blind man, who was in love with this girl, and he makes love to her using a language which is Braille, of course. And it takes place at twilight, at

dusk, and then ends at sunrise. The whole thing takes place at night.
DAC: So it preserves the classical unity of time, actually having the story unfold in one single day—although instead of a day, it happens in a night.

MGG: At night.

DAC: Why is night a preoccupation of yours? Not preoccupation—that's probably the wrong word.

MGG: Well, it is, in a way.

DAC: But it seems to be something that's a source of a lot of your imagery. There's a lot of night.

MGG: Well, it's very romantic, don't you think?
DAC: Certainly.

MGG: I think that's probably—

DAC: Some of the best things happen at night.

MGG: That's right. There's a movie called *History is Made at Night*. It's an old movie from the thirties.

DAC: What a great title!

MGG: It is. [There's another movie from the thirties] called *Midnight*, and it's a comedy. It is the funniest and best-crafted comedy I ever saw in the movies from that time. *Midnight*. Have you seen it?

DAC: No, I haven't. But I do love classic movies.

MGG: Oh, I live on 'em.

DAC: So your novel *Conversation Between Twilights* was about a blind man?

MGG: Yes, who makes love to his girlfriend…at night! And a queer thing about it is that he has a real good friend who's a painter, and all he can paint are the faces of dead people. So there's the night again.

DAC: You consistently equate death and night, which is something—

MGG: The dark.

DAC: That's understandable. But I was thinking, now talking about [your lost novel with] the painter who only paints faces of dead people, and then "Ashes of the Dead": in your imagery, does anything particularly Mexican—

MGG: In Mexican tradition, in the Day of the Dead.

DAC: Do you feel like any of that—that awareness of the history and ancestry and heritage—do you think any of it makes its way into some poems?

MGG: I don't think so. I think death for me is something very personal and not cultural. You know, Tita, who is very folklore-oriented, when she was in San Antonio as director of the Mexican Cultural Institute, every November at the institute they would have this *Altar de Muertos*. And that's never been my own personal culture.

DAC: Is it because of your family?

MGG: My father was of Mexican and Spanish descent. My mother was Mexican, of German descent, and she was Protestant. And my father was, to the best of my understanding, an agnostic military man. So even though as a child I was encouraged to go to a Presbyterian church, and when I was in school, as a boy in San Antonio, we were supposed to go to church on Sunday, I'd just take off. I would take off to the railroad tracks.

DAC: It was a personal thing for your father. At the time of the Mexican Revolution, were socialist doctrine and the idea of rejecting religion pervasive at all?

MGG: As a matter of fact, my father was anti-Communist, but he was a socialist in a Mexican Nationalist way at the time of 1910, 1913, 1920, and always felt that the church was. . . .what do they call it? A millstone around Mexico's neck.

* * *

DAC: Clearly translation is vital to your poetry. I think that there are, practically speaking, a couple of layers of sensibility when it comes to translation: one is literalness, and the other is evocativeness. The capturing is not just in translating the language, but trying to render again the experience of the poem. To translate the poem, you have to replicate the experience.

MGG: Yes. I'm sure you've heard the idea that it takes a poet to translate a poem. But I'm not sure about that. I think it takes a *craftsman* to translate a poem. I think that translating *anything*, perhaps even a scientific treatise, but certainly poetry, takes craftsmanship. In other words, you have to render in a second language what was done in the first language.

DAC: Right. But *on the terms* of that language, because every language has its own rules as well as its own feats of prosody. Like in Old English, where we have alliterative verse: it's alliteration and not end rhyme because it's a highly-inflected language.

MGG: And Spanish. There again, you have the vowel rhymes, but not perfect rhymes, where you rhyme both vowel and consonant. And then the French had the *rime leonine,* which had to rhyme *two* words, not one.

DAC: Are there any poems that you've written, published or not, where you started out with the task of a challenge like that?

MGG: Oh yes.

DAC: And then you wrote *into* the form?

MGG: Oh yes, I think so. I think all the poems—well maybe not all, but many of the poems that I've done in strict form, whether it's the sonnet or simple quatrains, with meter and rhyme, are all about those challenges. There cannot be, except maybe, *maybe*, for one first line of verse that just flashes through your mind, what in Spanish we call a *lirismo*, a lyricism. But even then, if you want to follow that with the same length and the same sound, you've got to work at it. That's why there's even such a thing called a rhyming dictionary.

DAC: Have you ever written a sestina? Or similar forms?

MGG: In Spanish I've written more sonnets, for instance, and *décimas*, like the last one in *Nueve musas eróticas*. And incidentally, if ever I wanted to do that book in English, with the drawings—and drawings with color, which I have of this lady who died, the artist—it would have to be not nine muses but perhaps ten. Because you see, in the Spanish, it's a play on words. *Décima* is not only the tenth muse, it's the form of a *décima*, which doesn't exist in English. So I would have to write *another* poem to be *ten* erotic muses, and not nine. So form is always important to me.

* * *

DAC: Have you ever written poems or shared them with other poets and in a sense . . . I guess "workshop" might not be the right word.

MGG: Well, but a group thing.

DAC: Where you get suggestions and feedback?

MGG: I think long ago, mostly with graduate students, I had formed a group which met—you know, everything here has changed, not only in the University, but all around. Across the street from the Ransom Center there's a large building, and when it was first built, it had wonderful places. On the first floor there was more than one café, and shops, and so on. And that's where we met, these students and I. We were about six, no more than that—six, seven. And it was mostly for their benefit. They were wanting to write, and wanting to hear each other and have me listen to them and suggest improvements to their writing. And I read my work to them as well. That's one instance. Before that, when I was teaching at Bryn Mawr College, there was an older couple who brought together a number of people interested in poetry to read their own work and other people's work. And they published a little magazine as well. That was before 1965. That was in 1959, 1960 or so. So those have been my experiences in that regard. Like for instance with [the Texan poet, translator, and editor Dave] Oliphant. Although he's very private, too. Recently he published his autobiography. He's only seventy years old and what he's going to do the next ten years, I don't know. But besides his poems, he's also written two books on Texas jazz, which I found very interesting.

DAC: So you have engaged in communal thinking about your poetry, allowing, if you will, conversation to filter in?

MGG: Well, I guess in the last analysis, I think, poetry is, in some ways at least, if not totally, a "statemental" form of expression, rather than a discursive form of expression. I've told you about [Antonio] Machado. I told you Machado, saying in some writing that when philosophers come across what they themselves call a dilemma—Machado calls it being caught between the horns of a dilemma, or something like that—the philosopher wants to solve it, even if it's a dead end. He runs into a dead end, he can't resolve it. Machado says that at that point, he goes up to the roof, flies off the roof, or *to* the roof. That's where the *poet* can take over. But . . . as a poet myself, I tend to believe that the process is private.

DAC: That reminds me of Giambattista Vico.

MGG: Vico, yes.

DAC: Vico has written that in the hierarchy of thinkers and recorded thought, it's the poet *over* the philosopher: the "first . . . wisdom was poetic in nature." It's really poetry that produces history, as well as that which history serves. I think [George] Santayana put this into one of his aphorisms: "The function of history is to lend materials to politics and to poetry." But Vico said that the poet is the one, because he's not necessarily solving—

MGG: He's not restricted to the rules of reason.

DAC: Right. It's not through the laws of reason, syllogism or algebra. There's no burden of proof to produce the raw materials of "wisdom." But it's interesting Machado says [something like] this as well.

MGG: But then on the other hand, at some point, I forget in what work, because I haven't read him all, but Nietzsche says that poets lie too much. Simply because they work with images. Where do images come from? Where do they gel? *In imagination*.

DAC: You've given me some new poems, unpublished poems, that seem to be, in this vein, very philosophical in nature.

MGG: They are different from some of the others.

DAC: And these are very recent?

MGG: These are recent. And they have come, if not directly, indirectly from the Spanish. I think all of them. The one that's called "The Written Word" is out in a magazine from Tulsa, *Nimrod*. Or at least I'm told that it's out but I've yet to receive a copy.

* * *

DAC: If I may, I'd like to turn to a totally different subject altogether. Earlier you spoke about women in your life, relationships in your life. You seem to have an enviable ability to have relationships [with lovers] and have them not really sour, even if they end; they stay friendly, they stay good, they stay close. They even stay alive. But I was wondering: was there anyone who got away? Was there anyone that this *didn't* happen with? Maybe even when you were very young? And did any record related to this find its way into poems?

MGG: Well, there were girls I knew, and not necessarily any I wrote poems to or about. And those relationships were totally innocent. They were romantic, but it never reached the sexual. In some cases they were just casual, incidental, brief involvements. There were one or two others that were meaningful in that they constituted a sort of fascination. There was one girl whom I met when I was in high school, and then when I came to the university and she went to college in San Antonio, I would go to see her, and we had that relationship for I don't know how many years, quite a few—*years*, mind you. And we talked about getting married. Her younger brother always referred to me, "Well, you're gonna be my brother-in-law." She had a wonderful mother. But there came a time—I was in my senior year in college—and I guess, I don't know whether it was some kind of an anxiety to get something established for her future, or whether it was just that her friends and classmates were marrying, and she wanted to get married. And I said, "Look, I can't get married now, I've got to finish school. I don't have *anything*." Well, she took that *very* badly and very seriously. Not badly, because we remained friends, but nonetheless seriously. And she met somebody else, and married, and that was the end of that, and she had two children. I considered her a very beautiful girl. In essence, she was a kind of figure of fascination to me insofar as there was a context of innocent rapport.

DAC: Did you ever write about it?

MGG: Yes, in *Desert Sequence*. For one, there's the poem (very, very indirectly), "Dark Fisherman," where it says, "You I remember, slowly intimate / and smiling."

DAC: That's her?

MGG: That's her. And then in "I Have Repeated Many Times," the line "To a girl with lemon braids." She was blonde. There's another poem somewhere inspired by that relationship. There may be others. *Oh*—and by the way, in "I Have Repeated Many Times," there's mention of "This invitation to go on a trip"; one time when I went to visit her at that point, we had a date, we went out, and it came up about the business of marriage. I said, "Are you willing to elope?" And she said yes. "Well, let's do it"—acting crazy! And she said, "But let me go by the house. I want to leave my parents a note." I said, "No."

DAC: That's why you didn't elope?

MGG: Exactly. I said, "We either go, or we don't go, right now." So she wouldn't go without going by and leaving her parents a note. That's why we didn't go.

DAC: So you came—

MGG: *Close*. Very, very close. Well . . . that would have been different.

DAC: I'm sure.

MGG: Yes. This was around 1950.

DAC: What was her name?

MGG: Her name was Clara, but she liked to call herself Leslie.

DAC: But in this relationship, too, you maintained a friendship after.

MGG: Oh yes. In fact, she called me when I turned eighty. She said, "Do you know that I'm two years younger than you are?" I told her, "I thought you were *six*."

DAC: Is "Figures of Earth" about Leslie, too?

MGG: Yes.

DAC: Did you ever call her "Preciosa"?

MGG: No, that's Tita.

DAC: And who's Gabriella?

MGG: Oh, a friend who lives in Bologna, Italy—a doctor, not a physician. She has a doctorate in chemical biology or something like that from the University of Bologna.

DAC: And you met her at the University of Texas?

MGG: Yes, she was visiting here. And Tita and I have visited her in Bologna. She has her own apartment, and across the street she has another little apartment for guests. Lovely place, and lovely person. She's also very sensitive. I've published a chapbook for her here, because she speaks English very well, and has written verse. She plays the violin beautifully. She's an artist as well as a scientist.

DAC: Along those lines, there are some dedications of your poems that I'd like for you to explain. In *The Brandywine in Winter* you have "Hints of Perfection, Notions of Grace. . . . In memory of John Frederick Jansen."

MGG: He was a professor at the Presbyterian Theological Seminary here in Austin. Wonderful man.

DAC: How did you meet him?

MGG: I [audited] courses there, as a visitor, not for credit or with any intention of getting a degree or anything like that. He was one of the faculty members whose classes I attended, and we became friends. He died.

DAC: I'm also curious about "Mountbatten." What possessed you to write that poem?

MGG: His assassination. That's one thing I'd say to the IRA, "Their revolution has become a sham." Killing an eighty-aught-year-old man, who *really* had nothing to do with their problems: but he was a symbol.

DAC: *The Brandywine in Winter* also includes, "The Other Side of the Map . . . for María Kodama."

MGG: In the last year of his life, Borges married her, a woman of Japanese and Argentine ancestry. She was an Argentine—*is*—she's still alive. She was a student of his, and became kind of a secretary and companion. And then in the last year of his life, he married her. He had been married before, to a woman who was a . . . devil.

DAC: Before Kodama?

MGG: Before Kodama, yes. They divorced. And of course the story goes that for the longest time he was married to his mother, because he had not married until in late life.

DAC: So he was blind when he remarried.

MGG: Yes he was. And then they were together in Geneva. He died there. They had an apartment.

DAC: Borges came to the University of Texas, right? In 1960?

MGG: Well, he came several times. The first time he was here for a whole semester, but I wasn't here. I was still in the Northeast. Then after I came in 1965, he came a couple of times. I would pick him up at his hotel.

DAC: Do you think he had an effect on you as a writer?

MGG: I'm not sure. I really don't feel it right now. He had an effect on me as a person and as a writer, but not in my writing. For instance, I'm a great admirer of his poetry, which is far less popular than are his stories. But I think he was a wonderful poet. Traditional. But I was influenced more by Neruda, for instance.

DAC: You would call Neruda an influence?

MGG: Yes, definitely.

DAC: The love poems and the "Song of Despair"?

MGG: Yes. And the existentialist things in his collection of *Residence on Earth* [*Residencia en la tierra*]. Definitely. And that's not about love. But you see, in fact, I translated some of Neruda. I translated one of his poems from *Veinte poemas de amor*, the one that starts, "*Me gusta cuando callas*." And I used the line but changed it around in a poem for Tita called "Love Poem."

DAC: So many of the poems in *The Brandywine in Winter* have dedications. Another is "Out for a Ride."

MGG: The epigraph is from "Leaves" by Desmond Egan, whom I met here, by the way.

DAC: Why did the phrase "everything turning like traffic lights" strike you?

MGG: Well, sometimes poems are just suggested to you without it being clear why. What does the poem convey to you? Maybe I failed.

DAC: I'll read it. "Out for a Ride."

The houses glide by
Before the car comes to a stop.
And before it starts again,
You wonder who might live there
Or who might have lived there
Over the urban years.
Have they fallen by the wayside,
Which is to say save those who are actually there,
Have they gone to a better place?

So many times you stop to think
Only because your car has stopped
For a traffic light or a sign
That can mean much more
Than simply obeying a rule.
Moving is so like a river, the Liffey or Lethe,
When stopping then moving on.
The point being this:
It sometimes takes a machine
To make you think
Of others who may or may not
Be going anywhere.

MGG: I think it's a poem made of *almost*, you might say, double entendre. You wonder about a house: Is it inhabited? Is it not inhabited? If it's not inhabited, those who lived there, did they just leave, or did they die? And there's the cars stopping, the traffic lights, the signs meaning much more than stopping the traffic—that kind of thing.

DAC: So the passage of life, within the spaces of an urban landscape.

MGG: Of the urban type: there's that word used there, the urban. And then of course the Liffey is that [running through the center of

Dublin]. The Liffey is a reference to Egan being Irish, [coupled with the Lethe, the river of Hades] since the names of the two rivers sound alike.

DAC: "Written on a Timetable" is a poem I like very much, in memory of your father.

MGG: Yes.

DAC: In a way it also reminds me of two other poems: "The Country Nurse" and "Pregnant Girl with Dogs," with their shared sentiment, sensitivity, and sympathy. Does it seem like there might be connections between these poems, in terms of perspective and sympathy?

MGG: Even the style.

DAC: The style, too.

MGG: I can tell you about how they came about. I think we talked about "The Country Nurse" before, and that's mainly just a bit of imagination, having had the experience of living in the country, even though living in the country was just temporary. I inherited, as a matter of fact, from Betty, a farm in Central Texas, and it has an old farmhouse. And having gone there to spend time, sometimes it was almost a whole summer, sometimes it was just a week, but I got to feeling something about the moods of the climate, if you will, of a non-urban area, since we're so used to the urban. And so the business of "Written on a Timetable" was a very definite personal experience. I was still living in Pennsylvania, having gone to Princeton and then teaching at Bryn Mawr. And my father was very ill; when serving in the Mexican Army in southern Mexico, he contracted malaria. So he suffered from consequences in the liver functions all his adult life, and he died when he was seventy-seven years old. I've survived him long, as did my mother. Anyway, when he had another attack of his illness, he came to Texas to a clinic in Temple. They have a fairly famous medical clinic there called Scott & White. This was his last internment in hospital, because he died there. So as I say, I was living in Pennsylvania, and when he was so ill that my mother said, "You'd better come, because he may not pull out of this one," I took a train. (It was still in the days of the train. This is 1963, the same year that President Kennedy was assassinated.) I took a train and I found which was the closest stop to Temple. And so here's the metaphor: the end of a life, the end of a train trip, and everything is on a timetable. In fact, I really did write the poem on the back of a timetable, and that's where the title came from.

DAC: While you were on the train?

MGG: Yes.

DAC: As I said, that poem reminds me of a poem I really love, which is "Pregnant Girl With Dogs." It starts, "Modestly carrying the secret of the universe." That's a great line. I mean, that's *really* a great line.

MGG: I think so, too.

DAC: "Modestly carrying the secret of the universe." The metrics are good, as is the rhythm. It made me think about sympathy, because the line is followed by, "She walks so casually, a triumph over curse." I thought of her as being a humble girl. At first read, I felt maybe the initial image is of a peasant, but it ends with an urban image, with the line, "Vanishing at the sudden corner of the street."

MGG: Right.

DAC: For me, there was a transformation in reading it a first time, especially with her being with the dogs. The turn happens at the very end. In some strange way the scene is quite discrete, but with the final line, "vanishing at the sudden corner of the street," it becomes urban. Is it right to have the image in your mind of it being a humble girl?

MGG: Well, she's not a *peasant* girl—we don't say "peasant" in Texas—but, you know, a country girl, a farm girl? No, she's not that. It happened [in Austin], in fact, two blocks from my house. Betty and I bought a house in 1965, a house that my brother and sister and I had bought for my mother when she came from Mexico to live here, [. . .] so one day I walked two blocks to the corner grocery store. And as I was walking, approaching the store, I see this girl. Nice figure from the back. Then I noticed that she was pregnant. And she had two dogs on a leash. Now, what you might not know is what it says there after "the universe," and the rhyme is "curse."

DAC: Yes: why "curse"?

MGG: You don't know what that means in women's parlance? Every month they have "the curse." And having become pregnant, *that* has stopped. So it has those little playthings there.

DAC: That changes my reading of the first stanza.

MGG: And it's *not* a farm girl—it's a girl right here [in the city].

DAC: I figured that by the end when she vanishes at the corner of a street, a very urban image.

MGG: Ending on the word "street," yes.

DAC: And "the *sudden* corner of the street." Even the word "sudden" makes it feel a little more rapid and thus more urban. You have another poem, in *The Musicians*, for Stanley Burnshaw, called "Art of Poetry."

MGG: Yes. Do you know anything about him?

DAC: No.

MGG: He was a marvelous man. And I take pride in having introduced him to Tom Staley, the director of the Ransom Center—and Tom is a charmer. I mean, you know, to get Norman Mailer's archive, to get Don DeLillo, to get John Fowles (whom I recommended he pursue), and now he's trying to get Ian McEwan: to get these things, he's got to be a charmer. So he charmed the old man, terrific old man, Stanley Burnshaw. He was a poet, but he was also a literary promoter in New York. He had been so successful that he also had a house on Cape Cod or somewhere in Massachusetts, *and* a place in Florida. I think he died in Florida. And he was in his mid-nineties when he died. It was in this very room where one time he came to visit Austin, and we talked about that poem. That poem was—how many stanzas does it have now? Three?

DAC: Four.

MGG: Four. Well, I think it only had three, or it could have been just two—probably three. But from what he said to me about the poem, I decided to write the fourth stanza.

DAC: Which stanza was that, do you remember? The last one?

MGG: The last one.

DAC: I think Burnshaw made a good call because of the final turn to the now. The stanzas begin with, "Poetry, I once thought," "Poetry, I next thought," "Poetry, I then thought," and so "Poetry, I now think," completes the progression.

MGG: That's right.

DAC: And as poetry, etymologically speaking, is a making, a doing, *poesis*, it's effective to get to the present, to the end. That's something I really liked about it. Okay. "The Mirror's Face" is dedicated to Octavio Paz.

MGG: Yes.

DAC: It's an abecedarian, in a way, inside of two free verse stanzas, even though you have an interruption of the alphabetical sequence. Once you start the abecedarian, there's a question that interjects between "D" and "E," but the rest is intact, and then the final stanza. Why did you finish the poem with the interjection not keeping this intact? Why interject there? Should I read it again?

MGG: Sure. Incidentally, this was a challenge, because I did it in Spanish as well; since it was, of course, dedicated to Paz, the original was in Spanish. And to do it again in English, insofar as effort, was really demanding. In fact, read the version I have, and we can go through it line by line.

DAC: "The Mirror's Face."

There's no one there,
And yet we think we see
A world of entities
That would explain a content in a void,
An alphabet of images denoting
Conformations of beleaguered sights.

MGG: [That's the first stanza.] So, how can there be a content in a void? And then we begin the abecedarian.

DAC: Adam ribboned / angel aflame
Beauty's being Beelzebub
Chimera's chrysalis
Dream / delusion / doppelgänger

MGG: Then the break with the desiderata.

DAC: Is the mirror the reality
In which everything
Displays its falsehood?

MGG: So *you're* wondering why the question there. Well, I wanted to ask the question of myself, or, for that matter, of the reader, or of anybody. But I didn't want to keep running the abecedarian, and *then* having the question. In other words, having a suspense.

DAC: Erotic elf / Everyman's envy
Fiction / figment / fragment
Ghost or glorified gorgon
Hallucination (here = there)

MGG: We run into some problems here.

DAC: I (eye looking for illusion) / Icarus drowning
Jabberwocky Judas
Kairos and Kronos
Lilliputian logarithmic lacrima christi
Melusina's maelstrom
Nothingness

Orpheus singing
Pithecanthropus erecting
Quo vadis, Brutus?
Revenant's revery
Simultaneous simulacra
Tabula rasa (there = here)
Utopia
Vision's variation's vagary
Wraith / will-o'-the-wisp
X
You and yourself =
Zero

MGG: And then comes the development beyond the abecedarian.

DAC: And the urge goes on,

The effort to transcend,
To penetrate behind the veil of glass

MGG: This is a mirror—

DAC: To stir the staple underneath the steeple.
With chisel and with sword
To carve the curve of solid geometry,
Of unconventional creative skill and kill
Until the bones in darkening caves,
The nonexistent shells only imagined
Wear away,
Until the pecker-penis-pencil-pen
That prances on the page
Succumbs to crumbling senses
Of barren incapacity,
Of incredulity,
The prelude to the silence that portends
The infinite aloneness
Within a thrice abysmal,
Zany labyrinth of dictionaried thought
There in the mirror
Where no one is.

MGG: *I* find something missing from the Spanish, which is the original. In the Spanish, there's "the black mass." And "the crystal hymen." It's not here, but it's there [in the Spanish]. And I think *that* is the right poem.

DAC: The Spanish?

MGG: The Spanish. You know, this is one of the things that I maintain. In fact, I have it in the author's note of *Looking for the Horse Latitudes*, that the original is always the right text.

DAC: Well, as it appears in *The Musicians*, that poem is followed by

"Lindbergh."
MGG: Yes, although the sequence is not significant.

DAC: Okay. But is "Lindbergh" reaching back to memory or myth?

MGG: Myth, not memory.

DAC: You were an infant [when your father met Charles Lindbergh in Mexico City and presumably was permitted to fly *The Spirit of St. Louis* with you sitting in the plane with him].

MGG: Yes, I was a year and a half or something like that.

DAC: You invoke mythology with Icarus. So this is a family *myth*?

MGG: It's family mythology, exactly.

DAC: It's probably not true that you flew in *The Spirit of St. Louis* with your father? Or do we just have no recourse to know? To have flown in that plane, given the circumstances, sounds a little iffy.

MGG: I have the recourse of having been told so by my father and mother.

DAC: Oh, okay, *they* told you.

MGG: Yes. But I have no proof, so to speak, because they're gone.

DAC: I understand. There's also the poem "Horowitz"—

MGG: Oh, let me tell you, since we're talking about experience and history and so forth: the poem "Lindbergh" was written in this very room [in the Ransom Center]. The poem "Horowitz" was written a day or two after Hazel and I watched at her house a program of [the Russian pianist Vladimir] Horowitz, having returned to Moscow for the first time in his life, I guess. He was already so old. It was such a great ovation he received. We watched him playing on television. Then, as I say, a day or two after, I had some reason to drive to the farm, which as I told you I inherited from Betty and her family, in Central Texas outside of a town called Gatesville. I don't know what time I left, but I remember stopping at a town called Salado, which is on I-35. There's a wonderful place there to eat called the Stagecoach Inn. So I stopped there to have a late breakfast, and while I ordered, while I was being waited on, I kept thinking about the experience of watching Horowitz. I'm always so impressed by musicians and singers. And I happened to have some paper, or maybe I used a napkin—I can't remember—but the idea came to me, "I've got to write something about Horowitz *right now*." So there, at the Stagecoach Inn, I wrote "Horowitz." Vladimir Horowitz. There's another great pianist who's named also Vladimir—Ashkenazy.

DAC: The image of Horowitz's hands ranging across the keys as "Two unimaginable spiders" is very evocative. This cluster of poems in *The Musicians* is quite explicitly related to musicians. "Singers and Sinners" begins "While listening to Bjorling, / Thought like theme crosses angelically / My mind." Is [Jussi] Bjorling a favorite of yours?

MGG: He surely was. He was a Swedish tenor. And as an undergraduate here, when I was still unmarried—which means before 1956—I heard that Jussi Bjorling was coming to San Antonio to sing at an opera. I made up my mind that I was going to go hear him, even if I had to go by myself. So the day came, I got in my car, and I took off. This was long before I-35 was built. So I went on the old highway, what was the Austin-San Antonio Highway, Highway 81. I got to the Municipal Auditorium in San Antonio, in time to get my ticket, I went in, sat down, and waited. And finally this man comes out, addresses the audience, and he says, "We regret to say that Mr. Bjorling will not be able to sing today, and his understudy will have to take over." Later I found out that Jussi was drunk in his dressing room. He eventually died from drinking. He was a *marvelous* tenor. But I didn't get to hear him in person.

DAC: What a disappointment.

MGG: And that poem, you know, was a concoction of musical figures, all of whom died in the same year. Even Elvis is there. And [the soprano] Maria Callas, Leopold Stokowski. . . . Of course this was written much later than when I went to San Antonio to hear Bjorling, *way* after. He's mentioned because he was still one of my favorites—and because he died that year. Callas, Stokowski, Elvis. What I said about Elvis I think is something that I like: "Elvis, poor later rich boy, who changed so much / Around him, more than we really care to know."

DAC: Was there a famous piece that Bjorling was known for, or a particular composer that he sang? Unfortunately I'm not familiar with Bjorling, but I'm trying to get his mood, beginning to end.

MGG: Well, he doesn't remind me of anything like what they did later in the case of the three tenors, [Luciano] Pavarotti and Plácido Domingo and [José] Carreras. Bjorling was purely operatic, and in his recordings that are still available—he does Puccini so beautifully. One of the things that I like best, and Tita and I talk about this a lot because she knows music and art, is the duet, two women singing: a soprano and a mezzo, for instance. (Or, for that matter, two sopranos, or with men's voices, a tenor and a baritone.) I'm thinking now of the wonderful baritone, Sherrill Milnes, still living today, who did duets with Plácido Domingo. And with Bjorling, it was, oh, beautiful duets. He did some with [the baritone] Robert Merrill. Jussi Bjorling and Robert Merrill.

* * *

DAC: In *The Musicians* there's another poem, "Our Lives," with a dedication to Paul Patrick Rogers.

MGG: Paul Patrick Rogers was a professor of Spanish at Oberlin College for many, many years. When I came back to Texas as an assistant professor in 1965, I first met his son, Douglass Rogers. Douglass had been here only a year or two before I came. We became friends and still are. He's living; he's a year older than I am. Anyway, after so many years here, all of a sudden Doug told me that his father was coming to live in Austin. He had been a widower. Doug's mother had died and Paul had remarried, a woman *much* younger than he, a German. I don't know the history—I've never asked as to where he met her, and I don't know whether she had been an academic, too, or not. Why he picked Austin, I don't know—it wasn't because of his son living here. I guess maybe because of the university. In any case, at that time the department of Spanish and Portuguese had been flourishing. It was number one or two in the country. So, when we met, I formed a friendship with him which was different and separate from my friendship with his son, Doug Rogers. He wanted to read my poetry in Spanish—he didn't care about the English, because he was a Spanish professor. He had had an interesting life—in his heyday back in the thirties, he had gone to France, I guess it was, trying to get into Spain because of his ardent support of the Spanish Republic against [Francisco] Franco and his fascists. Well, he couldn't get a visa. He had an American passport, but he couldn't get a visa to get into Spain because the attitude of the US government toward Spain at the time was *very* ambiguous. They claimed to be anti-Hitler, anti-Mussolini and so on, but they were not officially anti-Franco. Nevertheless, he couldn't get into Spain. He went to the border in France and came back. So in order to satisfy his friendship and his feelings about Spain, Republican Spain, he took to going to Mexico and he met many of the Spanish exiles there: Luis Buñuel and some of the poets.

In any case, he wanted to read my poetry. And after he read quite a bit of it, he said to me, "There's something that worries me about your poetry." And I said, "Tell me about it, Paul." And he said, "Well, you're always talking about yourself in your poetry. There's always I, I, I." And I said, "By golly, that may be true. It's lyrical poetry, and the voice, the speaker has to be me." But I thought about that, the "I," when it came to writing the poem which I wrote for Hazel, "The Space of Night," which I wrote before she died when she was very sick. She had been sick for several years. The same thing happened to me with Betty—her death was not sudden, and lasted a long time. Anyway, when I started writing "The Space of Night," I started thinking of Hazel being sick, and eventually it was going to come to an end. I was also thinking of Paul Patrick Rogers telling me about "I, I, I." There's not a single first person pronoun. Well, there is the first person plural—"we." But there's not an "I" in that poem. It's funny that I was thinking of Paul's remark.

DAC: Why *were* you thinking of that?

MGG: Well, it was going to be a long poem. I *knew* it was going to be a long poem. And if I started out with "I," it would be repeated and repeated and repeated. And thinking that maybe other readers like Paul were going to find *some* objection to that, I said, "Well, you know, I don't have to do it."

DAC: So for "The Space of Night," as it reappears in *The Brandywine in Winter*, there's a dedication, "In Hazel's memory," but that's something that you added later?

MGG: Later. But I started writing it with her living.

DAC: You started it when she was living and you finished it after she passed?

MGG: No, no, I finished it with her still living. But because of the publication date of *The Brandywine in Winter*, I said "In her memory," because by that time she was gone. See, she died in '93, and this collection was published in 2004.

DAC: That reminds me: *Desert Sequence* was published in '56, and then your next monograph in English was '84. Is that right? Even though you'd been writing all that time? And I think that that volume from '84, *The Infinite Absence*, has poems written in the fifties.

MGG: Yes. Poems that I was actually putting into print were mostly in Spanish. The jump in English is a long jump.

DAC: *Palabras inútiles* was published in '88—

MGG: *En vísperas de olvido* comes after *Desert Sequence*.

DAC: Right, in '67.

MGG: *Palabras inútiles* comes even later.

DAC: The published version of *Palabras inútiles* does not have the same dedication as your manuscript form.

MGG: That's right, because a friend of mine did that for me, and he left out the dedication. I guess he just wanted to do it very simply. It's not a very good reason, but I think the reason was that he didn't find a way of reproducing the pictures.

DAC: The two images?

MGG: Yes. I mean, he could have put a little note, but he didn't.

DAC: The manuscript has a picture of Betty, and that other image was—

MGG: A color etching by a French artist, Yves Ganne.

DAC: Okay. To return to Paul Patrick Rogers, did his comment about the "I" affect more than just that "The Space of Night"?

MGG: No, not really. Of that poem, I said, "It's going be long; what am I going do?" And then I remembered what he had said. It didn't affect me *very* much, really, but it did strike me at the time.

DAC: Also, the poem's not about you.

MGG: That's right.

* * *

DAC: How did the 2007 publication of *Looking for the Horse Latitudes* come about?

MGG: Joe Bratcher [at Host Publications] called me and he said he wanted to do a book, but it had to be in two languages.

DAC: So it was his idea?

MGG: Yes. I felt that poems from a different collection, *Nueve musas eróticas*, would be the most appropriate because as a collection it is the best, but at that time I had not considered finding a way to put in English *Nueve musas eróticas*. That came as a thought later, *also* from Bratcher, because Dave Oliphant told him that he had read that collection and thought it was great. So he said, "Let's do that one instead." I said, "No, not yet." The reason was, actually…well, two reasons. One reason is that I think *Looking for the Horse Latitudes* is more representative, because it has poems on many things. The other reason is that I didn't *want* to translate *Nueve musas eróticas*. I did finally translate one of the poems from that collection [for the magazine the *Dirty Goat*] but I don't know what response he did in fact get because I have not communicated with him since I sent it to him. He's published some daring things.

DAC: What are some of the differences between *En busca de las calmas ecuatoriales* and the English version of *Looking for the Horse Latitudes*?

MGG: Well, to begin with here, "*Cenizas de los muertos*," and "*Tenochtitlán*," which I left out because I thought that the English would not hold very well. Its dedication is for Andrea Córdova, who was a friend of Tita's and mine. She was a sculptress, and she was assassinated—murdered, actually, by a lover of her mother's. The mother had died, and this man wanted her inheritance, and he thought that Andrea, being the daughter, would come first, so if he got rid of her, he could argue for himself.

DAC: Wow.

MGG: Gruesome.

DAC: On the subject of that poem: I asked before if any sort of folklore or mythology from Mexico comes into play in your poetry, and you said no. But this one does.

MGG: This one definitely does, but somehow I think poetically the text wouldn't really hold too much in English. For one thing, it would require people to know the name of Tenochtitlán. Anyway, I left it out. I also left out "*Telenémesis*."

DAC: Which is dedicated to Verónica Castro.

MGG: She is still—of course we all get along in years—a very successful actress, especially on television. That's why the *tele*: the *tele* comes from television, and *nemesis*, because she's my undoing in my imagination. I think that this is one of the best poems I've written. But who in the United States would know, number one, who Verónica Castro is, not having lived in Mexico? That would lead to two, readers asking, "What the hell is *telenemesis*?" It wouldn't work in English, in my estimation. But it has some of the best lines. So anyway, so much for "*Telenémesis*." I did keep "*Naufragio*," the "Shipwreck," which gives the section its title, "Shipwreck with Mermaids." I think that one is another example of successful prosody, in both languages. And then comes "*A Safo*" ["To Sappho"]. In Spanish, I like it. In English I fairly well like it, but the end doesn't come out, because in order to translate literally what is said there, textually at the end, the English would have to use the word "whinnying." That's not a very poetic word. Whereas "*relincho*" is something else. As for the idea of this poem, for ages I've been fascinated with the figure and the fragments of Sappho. So that's the idea behind that.

And then comes, of course, "*Giovinezza*." Italian has another word for youth, *gioventù*, but I like the sound of *giovinezza*, even though it was the title of a hymn or march or something of Mussolini's fascists who were saying, "A new era of youth." It was, of course, at the same time that everybody was thinking of a new world, with all the scientific advances and inventions and how that shaped politics.

DAC: For the Spanish poems that have some folklore in them: was that reason for you not to translate or include them in the English version of *Looking for the Horse Latitudes*?

MGG: Well, it's my thinking that *because* of that folklore element, they're not going to be sufficiently understood by an exclusively English reader of poetry who has not had sufficient experience of Mexico through study or travel. And I hate for a poem to end up being, you might say, forced. That's how I feel about it. I may be wrong; somebody might say, "Well, let them go look it up!" Well, that's not good. I don't even like footnotes!

DAC: The problems come, or the impossibilities show up, when you just don't have the right word that carries both the music *and* the meaning.

MGG: Exactly. Or even a sense of discovery in the language, because I think that the poet, *rather* than an inventor, is a discoverer of the possibilities of language. That's why I say that when I write I kind of let the language lead me, like Don Quixote letting Rocinante take whatever road he wants.

DAC: You've translated a number of writers. Is it different to translate another author than it is to translate yourself?

MGG: Somewhere in the author's note of *Looking for the Horse Latitudes* I have something to say about that: "So the challenge generally faced by the translator of poetry is fairly well known. But the challenge faced by a poet in trying to replicate his or her own poetry in another language (assuming he or she is equally adept in both languages) is another matter. Any translator must be careful not to translate literally and yet, at the same time, keep the spirit of the original in the new version of what linguists call the target language. By spirit here I refer to the aura of impression, such as it may be, suggested by the original poem when heard or read. The ambilingual poet (as I regard myself) dealing in the transcription of his or her own poetry, though one would assume able to take more liberties, ends up having more trouble in fashioning equivalents. He or she might even be tempted to change radically some or all found in the patch of lyric that was the original. And that is because such poet happens to be uncommonly capable of navigating in the waters of two different languages, both poetical. This is uncommon because he or she must possess what in German is called *Sprachgefühl* (the feeling for a language) in two different realms of expression."

I think, for instance, of what I translated of [Spanish Nobel laureate] Vicente Aleixandre. I worked very hard on his translations, as you can imagine. But when I thought that I had grasped what he was saying, once I had done that, I didn't go into the possibilities of what *else* he might have said—whereas when I translate my own poetry, I do. "What else might I have said? How else could I have said it? Why did I say this?" And that's why in my chapbook in Spanish, *La lengua fracturada* ['The Fractured Tongue'], what I express there really is putting into question the efficacy of the poetic tongue, of the poetic word. How much does that language of poetry tell someone else, and how much is left unsaid?

Poetry ultimately is something made up of words. I don't want to give the idea that I'm thinking in terms of ambiguity, because that means that something went wrong. Although what is sometimes called polysemic may be there. I think that the reader of the poem, without necessarily thinking, or better yet being certain that he or she understands what that poem is, gets something out of it. That's the important thing. That's why I think that poetic language is the language of suggestion—not of unequivocal or univocal meaning. And furthermore, because of the sound and rhythm and music, it might suggest things that the poet himself might not have been aware of. Always an interesting experience for me is rereading and saying, "Hmm, this is not really all that good," and yet I must have thought it was at one time or else I wouldn't have put it there. I think the poet has the right to revise as well as the right to change his mind and criticize. Self-criticism is important.

DAC: When it comes to translation, in poetry so much relies on connotation as opposed to denotation. Do you find it's difficult to have a feel for that? And how far can you stretch connotations? Because connotations can be so cultural.

MGG: Well, sure!

DAC: Perhaps they're *entirely* cultural. Although sometimes they're linguistic, like the word "evening." So sometimes they are linguistic, but other times they're cultural.

MGG: Yes.

DAC: How do you handle that when translating—when you run into terms of connotation that resonate within Spanish language or Mexican culture? How do you replicate or approximate this sort of thing in some way in English?

MGG: That's probably the hardest thing in the world to do. I guess we would have to start with evaluating or analyzing the two languages in their "gross nature" and their development. English, I feel, is a much more dynamic language than Spanish. Not in the same way as German, but it is capable of coming up with words that are combinations. Now, Spanish can do that sometimes, but in an ordinary everyday sense, Spanish doesn't do that, because it would have to be a learned exercise. Whereas in English, every grocer can use language which is complex, because the language allows itself to change and grow. Things are constantly being created, of course, and advertising does all kinds of crazy things. And [before you know it] the whole world is saying it. Buzz words. How about buzz words? Spanish has, of course, popular expressions. In Spanish, they do funny things. And it will be interesting to see if parallel things happen in English. For instance, you're sitting at the table and you ask your mother or your brother to pass the salt, and you say, "*porfa*" for "*por favor*." And sometimes in order to lighten what would otherwise be a coarse word, such as *cabrón*, they say "*cañón*." But everybody knows that they mean *cabrón*. But the sound, you see, to the rhyme, *cabrón/cañón*, allows it to substitute. So both in the erudite language and in the *very* popular language, all languages *have* to be dynamic, but English, I think, is more dynamic than Spanish. I think Spanish preserves more of its old practices and even its old rules. Think of the structure of words in the two languages. English is almost a monosyllabic language, and when you're using long words in English it's because they were derived from Latin or French or something of the sort. Whereas with Spanish, you use a lot of long words.

DAC: In English, have you ever wished that it was gendered? For example, that there was an "el" and a "la"?

MGG: To learn that from scratch takes a while, whereas for a child, the Spanish-speaking child—what turns out to be a Spanish-speaking child—it just comes natural. The business of gender across the languages can be tricky. So often it happens that I will find somebody who wants to be friendly and say something that's like Spanish to me because they know that I speak Spanish. And so they think that you have to say "no problemo." How can you tell them that, yeah, *problema* is masculine, but it ends in "a" because of the Greek background?

DAC: Have you ever tried to find a substitute for gender in English? If you have a poem in Spanish and you translate it into English, have you ever tried to capture something, as it's getting rendered into the new form, that plays on the most fundamental connotations of the language?

MGG: Give me an example of what you're thinking.

DAC: If you were going to say in English, "a sunset," you can't personify it as gendered in English.
MGG: No, you can't.

DAC: As a native speaker of Spanish, is gender in Spanish transparent to you? Do you not really see its features or opportunities for connotation?

MGG: No. I guess because I'm a native speaker. But because I'm a native speaker, I find it funny that somebody will say "el problemo." By the way, speaking of translation, don't let me forget that I offered you a copy of the new translation of *Don Quixote*. I've got it at home.

July 12-17, 2009
Austin, TX

Photo by Kate Marshall

David A. Colón is assistant professor of English at Texas Christian University. He received his PhD from Stanford University and was a Chancellor's Postdoctoral Fellow and Visiting Scholar in English at the University of California, Berkeley. He is the author of the novel *The Lost Men* and has published articles and reviews in many publications, including *Cultural Critique*, the *Journal of Latino/American Studies*, *MELUS*, *Studies in American Culture*, and the *Princeton Encyclopedia of Poetry and Poetics*.

Miguel González-Gerth received his PhD from Princeton University. He joined the faculty of the University of Texas in 1965; served as editor of the *Texas Quarterly*; is Special Consultant to the Harry Ransom Center; and is a board member of Humanities Texas.

Frederick Luis Aldama is Arts & Humanities Distinguished Professor of English at Ohio State University and winner of the Modern Languages Association's Prize in US Latina/o and Chicana/o Literary and Cultural Studies (2004).